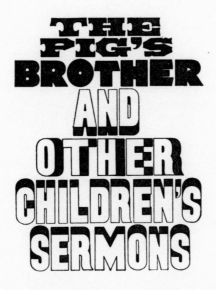

THE
PIG'S
BROTHER
AND
OTHER
CHILDREN'S
SERMONS

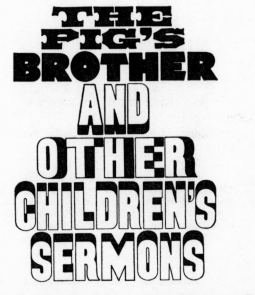

THE PIG'S BROTHER AND OTHER CHILDREN'S SERMONS

S. LAWRENCE JOHNSON

ABINGDON PRESS

NASHVILLE   NEW YORK

THE PIG'S BROTHER
AND OTHER CHILDREN'S SERMONS

Copyright © 1970 by Abingdon Press

Standard Book Number: 687-31423-2

Library of Congress Catalog Card Number: 79-97577

Scripture quotations unless otherwise noted are
from the Revised Standard Version of the Bible,
copyrighted 1946 and 1952 by the Division of
Christian Education, National Council of Churches,
and are used by permission.

SET UP, PRINTED, AND BOUND BY THE
PARTHENON PRESS, AT NASHVILLE,
TENNESSEE, UNITED STATES OF AMERICA

TO
ALICE

PREFACE

Fortunate is the church that has children attending the services of worship. These children should not be ignored. There is something about a sermon just for them that makes the youngsters feel as if they belong in the church.

These sermons for children have been written particularly for the child from eight to twelve years old, but may easily be adapted for younger boys and girls. Primarily, they offer ideas to present and are not just to be read to children attending church.

S. LAWRENCE JOHNSON

CONTENTS

FIFTY-THREE SUNDAYS
MAKE A YEAR

Among the many great gifts God has given you is the capacity to retain knowledge. This marvelous power we call memory. As with any faculty, some people are better equipped than others. In fact, some are very clever at being able to recall names and faces and things, quickly and easily. You can learn tricks to help you remember.

One of the ways to remember is by association. If you want to recall the name of Mr. Stone promptly when you see him, you are told to think of a huge rock; for Mr. Holland, you should see a tulip; for Mrs. Gardner, a shovel, and so on. Several years ago, when a minister moved into a new parish, a man said to him it would be easy for him to remember his name by association: "Although I'm thin, think of me as fat," he said. For months afterward the clergyman, every time he saw this man, thought of "fat," but could not for the life of him say "Mr. Stout."

Even before you started to go to school, I'm sure you heard two popular rhymes which are memory helpers:

> Red sky at night, sailors' delight;
> Red sky at morning, sailors take warning.

And,

> Thirty days hath September,
> April, June, and November;
> All the rest have thirty-one,
> Excepting February alone,
> Which hath but twenty-eight, in fine,
> Till leap year gives it twenty-nine.

You also learned that there are sixty seconds in a minute, sixty minutes in an hour, twenty-four hours in a day, seven days in a week and fifty-two Sundays in a year, didn't you? You know for certain there are exactly fifty-two Sundays in a year, don't you? There seem to be exceptions to all our rules. Usually there are fifty-two Sundays in a year, but every once in a while a year turns up with an extra Sunday. 1967 was one of those years with fifty-three Sundays.

The explanation for this extra Sunday occurring every so often is not too complicated. If I gave you a few minutes to think, you could probably come up with the answer. Every ordinary year—that is, a year which isn't leap year—begins and ends on the same day of the week. If a year begins on Tuesday, it will end on Tuesday; if it begins on Friday, it will end on Friday. When it begins on Sunday, it will end on Sunday. In 1882, 1899, 1905, 1922, 1939, 1950, and 1961 it began and ended on Sunday, so we had fifty-three Sundays in those years.

God has made this world of ours orderly. There is a plan, a systematic and predictable plan. This plan brings us a message which is well to remember at the beginning of every new year. All of us need to have an orderly plan for ourselves and our lives. You will find life easier and you will be much happier if you too have a system to follow, if you too set down rules for yourself.

In planning your set of rules for a new year, you will certainly want to include promptness as one of the most important on your list. To be fair to yourself and to other people you should be prompt. Another high on your list will be dependability. When you agree to do something, do it, and do it to the best of your ability. A dependable person is well liked.

Don't make your list too long. A short list will be much easier to stick to during the year. Day by day check to see how you measure up to your schedule. Practice makes perfect.

The poet Alexander Smith said: "A man's real possession is his memory. In nothing else is he rich, in nothing else is he poor." To make yourself rich with pleasant memories, pattern yourself in an orderly fashion as God does the universe.

LISTEN FOR THE VOICE

Overlooking Gloucester Harbor in Massachusetts is a beautiful statue called the "Gloucester Fisherman." It shows a man dressed in his oilskins, standing at the wheel of a ship. Looking directly ahead, his eyes are straining as if to see through the fog or the rain.

Since the founding of colonies on the eastern coast of the United States, many men have earned their livelihood at sea. Some have been fishermen, some have sailed the coastline, while still others have gone to the outermost parts of the earth in search of treasures.

One such old salt spent his retirement years in Salem, Massachusetts. His name was Captain Cunningham. For many years he had sailed a great four-masted schooner up and down the east coast. One time, on a run from Halifax, Nova Scotia, to Boston, he was perplexed by fog. It got so bad that by day it was impossible to see a quarter of the way up the main mast from the deck. For two days and two nights the captain was on deck without any sleep whatsoever.

At last he realized that he could keep on his feet no longer. After calling the first mate to take over, the captain went to his cabin. Things there were familiar and snug. It was warm and the lamp burned brightly. His cabin boy, seeing the captain come below, brought him a cup of steaming hot tea.

It was always Captain Cunningham's habit to "get on his knees" for a few moments before going to bed, "to just talk things over with the Admiral." As he recalled this particular experience he would say:

> I got down on my marrow bones and said: "Well Lord, it's up to you. I don't know where we are. You've made this ocean so darn big. We're on it and funny thing is, I know you know where. I can do nothing more. The ship and the men are in your hands, but if there's anything you think I can do, just call me and I'll get right up on deck again."

He lay down on his bunk and in a moment was fast asleep. Later he was told he had slept for about four hours. But let us listen to the captain again, in the words he used to tell the story:

> Must have been fast asleep because I felt someone holding my arm and shaking me hard. As I gained consciousness I heard a voice saying "Hey, Captain! Get up and to the wheel fast. Don't waste time arguing; I'll tell you what to do." I got me up there fast and grabbed the wheel and yelled, "Now what?" A voice clear and beautiful came through the fog crying, "Hard to the starboard!" and I swung the wheel over as far as she would go; a moment later we were aware of another craft passing us with not more than six inches to spare. The Admiral was on top of things and He told me just what to do.

15

Captain Cunningham used to delight in telling this story and would aways conclude:

So often we have our ears so filled with wax we can't hear, and don't want to do anything about it. But the Admiral speaks and tells us what's best for us. Unfortunately we often think we know best, and when we don't obey Him on the double, the crash can be dreadful.

VENTURE FORTH

Do you like hamburgers, hot dogs, peanuts, popcorn? Of course you do. Most people enjoy eating these foods. But have you ever tried eating pokeweed? You don't know what it is? It's a wild plant that grows to be about six to eight feet high. It has broad leaves and in the fall, tiny white berries which turn bright red.

In the South this is very popular among the country people. It requires little effort since you don't have to plant or cultivate it. You strip off the leaves from the stalks, wash them, and boil them in a little water. After they cook for a few moments, you pour off any remaining water and fry them with green onions. They make a delicious, filling vegetable. But because it costs nothing and is so easy to pick and prepare, many people will not even try the taste of pokeweed.

Many things keep people separated. Language is one of the greatest barriers to friendship between people of different nationalities. However, food habits and tastes are also a deterrent. One of the strongest factors keeping the Hebrew people together as a specific group has been their food habits. As America was becoming populated, cities were often divided into sections by nationalities—Germans were in one group, Italians in another, Irish in a third, and so on. It was extremely difficult for people belonging to any one of these ethnic groups to break away and come to the other. In many cases they were afraid the food they would be served would be tasteless or bad tasting or would upset their stomachs.

There has been much talk about not being able to feed all the people as our world rapidly becomes overpopulated. There is undoubtedly enough food, and will continue to be plenty, if everyone tries to venture forth in acquiring a taste for new and different foods. If you are offered pokeweed, try it. Don't say, "I don't know what it is; I've never tried it; I don't like it; it's only for southern people to eat."

Venture forth in gaining new friends too. Don't be afraid when you meet youngsters whose skin is a different color or whose parents come from a different country from the one yours did. Try to discover what you have in common instead of what distinguishes you. Just as it is fun to try different foods—frijoles, tamarinds, tangelos, gumbo, and thousands of others—so it is interesting to get to know other people. There are Chinese, Japanese, Koreans, Africans, Spaniards, Swiss, French, and so many more. Some foods you won't like at all; others you may like, but more of them you will find you enjoy.

We were all created by the same God. The psalmist wrote: "It is he that made us, and we are his." You will find that, as with food, most of the people you will get to know you will enjoy.

HEAVEN SCENT

The sense of smell is one of God's great gifts. Sight permits us to look out upon the world and appreciate color and shape. The ability to make sounds with the voice allows us to describe what we see in order that others may appreciate what comes to our attention. Although the sense of smell is just as valuable as these two, many do not develop this sense to the extent they might. Our breathing is automatic, and unless we make a conscious effort or unless scents are very strong, either bad or good, we pay little heed to them. With effort and concentration you can become aware of odors; some are very delicate and give you great pleasure, and others may warn you away from something dangerous.

The faint odors of cooking food or fresh fruit and vegetables give great joy. One can often tell what something is by simply smelling, without the need to look or handle it. We sometimes play a game of passing a little bag filled with spices, herbs, or odorous fruits and then try to recognize them by their smell. Have you played this game?

Riding through the countryside, occasionally we catch

the odor of a skunk. Certainly when it is fresh and strong very few would say they like it. The skunk has very powerful glands from which this evil-smelling yellow liquid can be pumped with such force that it can be propelled from eight to twelve feet, and sometimes farther. This is entirely under the control of the animal. It can throw this stench at will.

Skunks can make wonderful pets. Most people who domesticate them have these offending glands removed by a veterinarian; but this is not absolutely necessary, if you can be sure you will never frighten the animal. For this is the means of protection God has given it. The skunk is a quiet little beast and simply seems to be unable to fight and do many of the things other animals are able to do for protection.

There is also a small beetle which lives in the deserts of the southwestern United States which, like the skunk, can throw a stinking fluid. It is called "Eleodes longicollis." It doesn't fly and can move only very slowly. Ants, lizards, and other beetles would often like to eat these little bugs, but they have their protection. They can stand on their heads, pull the trigger, and the results are effective.

Humans don't need such protective methods. Humans do, however, fight with one another. But there shouldn't be any need to do so, because if they learn to live in love with others, fighting would be unnecessary. Men usually fight because they want something someone else has; we speak of the "haves" and "have nots." Men are greedy. Often they don't need what they fight to get. Really, there is plenty of everything; but some people insist on hanging on to what they don't need. They refuse to remember the words of Jesus: "Do unto others as you would have them do unto you."

____A STRONG HOLD____

You all recognize this as a kite. Under the proper conditions it will fly. But these conditions are very important. Without any of them this is but a bit of paper and a few sticks.

There must be a wind. What is wind? You can't see it. But you can feel it. It is a movement of air. This movement of air may be gentle and soft, or it may be harsh, strong, and destructive. I know you have walked down the street and felt as if the wind would blow you away. It would if you weren't sufficiently heavy to stay on the ground. Sometimes you have to hold your mother or father's hand so that they can add to your weight and help you to stay put!

Wind can lift and move things. Every year tornados in the South and the Midwest lift houses and barns, schools, and all kinds of things and carry them away, sometimes for miles. A soft wind carries things too: the dead leaves from the trees and the rain to places where it is needed. In life it is ideas, hopes, desires, and wants which are like the wind. These stimulate and encourage us.

Some things are necessary before you try to fly a kite.

You must be sure of the direction from which the wind is coming, so that you can launch your kite into the wind. If you try to go with the wind, your kite will not get off the ground. You must be sure you are as free from obstructions as you can be. In other words, you must make the proper preparations insofar as you are able. There are so many difficulties in life that we could avoid, if we would but take the trouble to make the proper preparations for what we want to do. But so often we are like the man who ran off in all directions at the same time.

A kite may fly high up into the sky. It can soar, twist, and turn. It is such fun to fly a kite. A kite has a body to catch the wind. It is made of strong paper or cloth, fastened to sticks of wood. But the kite must also have a tail. This gives the kite equilibrium, as your parents would say. Or rather, it keeps the top half pointing upward so that the surface of the kite is always pressed outward by the wind. But there is something else—a string. A kite cannot fly without a string. It is what gives the kite discipline. You don't like it sometimes when mother or father tells you that you can't just go off and do as you like, when you like. Yet discipline is absolutely necessary if you are to grow and develop properly.

There are all kinds of discipline. For example, there are what are called mores—those things that people have found good for them over long years. These work out in laws. Some of these laws are enforced by the state, but the more important ones are only enforced if we do so in our own lives. Then there is our religion. This is the discipline we set up for ourselves, based on what we believe about God. Much of what we accept about God comes from the teaching of Jesus.

So, rather than try to escape discipline, as some of us do, we should be happy we have it. Instead of trying to find ways around discipline, we should invite more of its firm pressure and be grateful.

A love of God and a desire to behave as we think he wants us to is the most worthwhile and valuable discipline a boy or girl, man or woman, can have.

LET THERE BE LIGHT

All of us recognize that this is a flashlight. How many uses there are for one! First, we use it to find our way in the dark so we won't stumble and fall and hurt ourselves. It is of equal value also for many other things. It can be used for sending messages at night, for showing others where we are if either we or they have become lost. A flashlight may be used for seeking things we want or need. You may have dropped a dime or even a contact lens, and you must have a close light immediately to help find it. What is better than a flashlight? A flashlight, too, will allow us to direct light into enclosures, such as dark holes; or if we are working with machinery and drop a nut, or bolt, or washer, the flashlight then becomes invaluable.

How does a flashlight work? What are its parts? There is necessarily a source of power, which is usually a battery. I had a flashlight once though that was operated by a small hand generator. There must also be a case to hold the source of power and for us to grasp while using it. There is a bulb or lamp which contains a filament made up of a material which sets up a strong resistance, making it glow brightly, giving off powerful light. Finally, there is a reflector.

The power source of life is God. It is God who made us, and it is God who gives us strength for living. It is God who gives us the energy and desire to accomplish. If the spirit of God is allowed to work in you, there is absolutely nothing you cannot do. Jesus said: "I do not speak on my own authority; but the Father who dwells in me does his works." God is the source of everything.

The universe is the case. God is self-contained within the universe which he has made. He is neither confined to this world of ours, nor to any particular one of the planets. Nor is he in any one of the stars that fill the night sky. Rather, his spirit pervades all and gives meaning, stability, and purpose to all.

Christ is the bulb or the lamp. It is in him that the power of God shows most surely. He is the point of brilliance in the life of man. He is the source of light to this world. It is he that can illuminate the dark corners, penetrate the deep holes of distress and despair. As the lamp in the flashlight glows with the concentrated essence of the energy of God, so Christ becomes that light which may be the light of the world. You must turn on the flashlight, you must use it. Likewise you must avail yourself of the Christ-light. It will not force itself upon you or anyone. It must be accepted and used with joy.

You are the reflector. The light of Christ, to help men out of their darkness, must be projected. This is your task and mine. Your lives must be so organized and developed that men may see what is good by your example. Jesus once said that a city which is set on top of a hill cannot be hidden, but can be seen by everyone. So, don't hide your light under a box, because if you do, no one can see it. Put it up high so that it can be seen and noticed by everyone.

If you paint the outside of a light bulb black, it wouldn't be of any value, would it? You wouldn't be so foolish as to do anything like that, I know. But there are a lot of people who do not sufficiently appreciate what the love of God, through Christ, can do for them, and so they keep his spirit hidden, or tightly locked up within themselves.

God said: "Let there be light," and Jesus said: "Let your light so shine before men, that they may see your good works, and glorify your Father which is in heaven."

DIRTY

New Orleans is a most interesting city to visit, particularly that part known as the "French Quarter." Much of this section hasn't changed greatly during all the years of its existence. The streets are narrow. The buildings are old and dirty.

The history of this area is exciting. The pirates Pierre and Jean Laffite walked these streets. Bowie, about whom the television stories have been written, lived here. Wax statues of these men may be seen in the famous museum which tells stories of New Orleans. There is also a figure of a beautiful young woman who tortured her slaves. She would have them chained in the attic of her house and would then herself beat them with whips and chains. She was finally driven from the city by her neighbors.

There are wonderful places to eat. There is a little French coffee shop where there are expensive but marvelous pastries for sale. Some big people, grown-ups, like the coffee that is served; but most of the little people find it too strong and bitter. You might take a mouthful to taste it and then really want to spit it out; but you would be too polite to do this and you would swallow it, but not like it at all. At any rate you could say you had tasted it, strong, black, and made with some stuff called chicory in it.

The convent and old Roman Catholic Cathedral you would like. They were at one time very beautiful, but now look a little bit the worse for wear.

At night there are lots of lights and jazz. It is all very gay and exciting.

If you have never lived near the sea, a visit to one of the fish markets is a must. There is a strong smell of fish. Inside the building there are many varieties for sale. There are big fish, little fish, white fish, red fish, yellow fish, shellfish of all kinds. There are shrimp, big ugly-looking lobsters, and many crabs.

Yes, the buildings are old and dirty, and as you walk down the streets your reaction would probably be: "My, I am glad I don't live in one of them. Why don't people do something about fixing them so they look clean and nice?"

But please don't be so hasty in your judgment. If it were possible for you to go into one of these houses you would be surprised. Perhaps the most dilapidated-looking house from the street is very beautiful inside. It may very likely be filled with wonderful old furniture. The drapes at the windows may be very lovely and expensive. The floors may be of exquisite, polished hardwood and the rugs colorful and thick.

In back of many of these houses are marvelous gardens with all sorts of beautiful flowers. Sometimes in the middle of a garden courtyard a fountain is throwing up cascades of water, which, as it catches the sunlight, looks like millions of diamonds.

So often boys and girls or men and women are apt to judge things and people by the way they look on the outside. This may be a mistake. Sometimes people may be ill and crippled and look horrible, but this does not mean that they are not beautiful characters. Jesus said: "Judge not, that you be not judged. For with the judgment you pronounce, you will be judged." We must be very careful when we meet a person that we do not make up our minds about them wrongly. First impressions are often deceiving.

THE LESSON
OF TWO POTS

Many years ago, perhaps more than five hundred years before the birth of Jesus, there lived a man named Aesop. He looked at the common things around him and saw they all had lessons to teach him. Fortunately for us, he was able to write and put his stories into words so that we can read them today.

Aesop was a slave. He was somehow killed by the people of an ancient Greek city called Delphi. We don't know exactly what happened. Perhaps it was through jealousy of his ability to understand and write. One of his greatest stories and best known is "The Frogs Desiring a King." This story, it is thought, was told for the purpose of dissuading the citizens of Athens from getting rid of the ruler they had and trying to find another to replace him.

Aesop also told a story about two pots. One was made of brass and the other of clay. It happened that these two pots came to lie on the bank of a stream. The rains came and the stream flooded its banks. The two pots began to float down with the current. The earthenware pot shouted to the brass pot to keep away from him. The brass pot answered that the clay one didn't need to worry for it would not bump it. The earthenware pot then said, "Whether I hit you, or you hit me, I shall suffer for it."

The lesson generally attributed to this fable is that we should be careful of the company we keep. However, to me there is another lesson, too: if we hurt another person we also cause damage to ourselves. If you hit a boy or a girl, if you take something that doesn't belong to you, if you say something that is untrue about another, or hurt them in any way, try as you will you cannot forget it, and you feel bad. Adults call this having guilt feelings.

There are people who study the way in which our minds work. They are called psychologists. They tell us that these feelings of guilt can do us very great harm. Did you ever see acid put on a bit of metal? This acid looks harmless enough, but the minute it touches the metal there is a lot of smoke and hissing; and the first thing you know, the metal has been eaten away and loses its strength. So these guilt feelings we get from having harmed another take away some of our strength and character.

There was another very wise man who lived long before Aesop. He was Solomon, who was a king in Israel. In the Bible we have a collection of wise sayings, many of which are thought to have come from Solomon. One of the things he was supposed to have said long ago is, "He that walketh with the wise men shall be wise: but a companion of fools shall be destroyed." Aesop may have known these words. I'm sure he would have accepted them, for they point out the same thoughts as he did with his story of the two pots.

31

___"YE ARE THE LIGHT___ OF THE WORLD"

Did you ever try to catch fireflies? A little boy came to me the other day with a half dozen of them in a glass bottle. He had made holes in the cap and put grass in the bottom of the jar. He really wanted to be as kind to the little insects as he knew how. He told me that at night they made the jar so lovely and gave so much light, that he was able to see words on a bit of paper when he held it near the glass.

Often at night you will be startled by seeing a little bit of green-blue light appear from nowhere and disappear almost as soon as it seems to have come. If you are quick enough, you may catch one of these bugs. God has given these flies the power to generate their own light. Some fish have been given similar power. These are called electric eels, and they can give an electric shock powerful enough to kill a man.

Years ago, one night Jesus was on the shore of Galilee with some of his friends. It was very dark. He looked up toward the ancient city of Safed. This old city is the northern-most town in Upper Galilee. It sits on a hill about 840 feet above sea level. This doesn't seem very high until you realize the lake is way down below sea level. Jesus called the attention of those who were with him to the lights of the city and said, "A city that is set on a hill can never be hid."

One night I was sitting on the shore of the Kinneret, which is what they call the Sea of Galilee in Israel. Kinneret means harp. If you study a map of this lake you'll understand why it is called by this name. It was a very dark night and the city of Safed shone like a bright star above us. Safed is one of the most sacred cities in Israel, and many wise men have lived there. An old saying about this city tells us: "In Safed is the purest air of the Holy Land, and there is not a place where you can understand better the secrets of the Holy Law."

So when Jesus called attention to this town, those who were with him thought not only of the physical light they could see shining from it at night, but also of the wise people from whom the light of knowledge and of the spirit was shining too.

The Master continued by saying: "You are the light of the world." Each of us has some contribution to make, some knowledge that might be of advantage to another. But there are some people who keep everything to themselves. We must not be selfish when we have something, or know something, that might be helpful to another.

In the sixteenth century, the first printing press in the land of Israel was installed in Safed, and here in 1578 the first Hebrew book was printed. Up until that time books had been printed by hand. This was like a shining forth of greater light of knowledge: "Let your light so shine before men."

"LET THE CHILDREN COME"

One of the delightful stories about Jesus tells of a time when he was with some of his followers out on a hillside. The disciples had many questions to ask. They wanted to discuss a lot of things which they considered of prime importance. Jesus stopped talking to the disciples and began speaking to some children who approached him. The disciples were upset, not understanding why Jesus would waste his time with a bunch of youngsters. But Jesus knew those children would be the men and women of tomorrow. He knew they needed love and attention and this need was, if anything, greater than the disciples' need for knowledge. So, when the disciples were going to send the children away, Jesus stopped them, saying: "Suffer little children, and forbid them not to come unto me: for of such is the kingdom of heaven."

You all have heard about George Washington. He was a general in the army, a wealthy farmer, a man who was supposed to have thrown a dollar across the Potomac River.

Yes, there is much we have heard about this man. But I wonder if you have heard this story?

One time when Mr. Washington was in a large northern city, far from home, he was invited to dinner. It was a cold winter night. Many guests had gathered together. The meal was prepared and ready to be served, but there was no Mr. Washington. The host had not seen him, for he had been away from home and had not arrived until almost the time when the guests were gathering. Everyone was disturbed.

One of the servants told the master of the household that the general had arrived some time before and had been shown up to his room, but had not returned downstairs. The master and servant went to the room that had been assigned to the general, but he was not there.

As they were about to return downstairs to inform the guests, they heard a man's voice singing: "Ride a cockhorse to Bambury Cross. . ." The sound was coming from the nursery. They opened the door and found the general, still in his dust-covered uniform, sitting and playing with the children. They were around him and over him. When the host saw this he was very confused, but didn't interrupt until the song was over.

General Washington laughed when he was told the guests were waiting, saying that it had probably done them good to wait for a change. He added that he would be down immediately, as soon as he had tucked the children into bed.

All of us are important, children and adults—we all want and need attention. It's a shame when a person gets "so big" that he is interested only in himself and doing those things which will bring him glory. The guests were people General Washington needed for support, but the children needed his love and he gave it. It is a great man or woman who recognizes the common things of life that give pleasure.

WHY WAIT?

As you grow older you will notice that we often have to make mistakes before we learn. My own children often say they have to "learn the hard way." I don't think they are much different from everyone else. But I guess there are some of us who learn harder than others. We are told to fasten our seat belts in our cars before we drive, but there are many mothers and fathers who do not fasten their own, and perhaps never think to insist that the children do until someone gets hurt.

For some time we lived in a town where people were very slow to shovel snow from their walks during the winter. One man said to me when I commented on this, "What's the difference, it'll melt!" One day a lady was trying to walk in front of his house after a snowstorm, and she slipped and fell, breaking both arms. This woman was not vengeful, but she thought since it was this man's fault, for not having cleaned the snow and ice from his walk, he should pay for her doctor's bills. He refused to do it willingly, so the court made him. He now shovels his walks immediately after every snow.

When the first railroads were built in England, tracks were laid across the countryside. Many times these tracks had to cross over roads. The only warning that the train was coming was from the "driver," as he was called, blowing on a little horn. This didn't make very much noise and often simply was not heard. When a cow would get on the track, the driver would blow his horn, but it was so faint that the cow often paid no attention. Poor cow.

One day in 1833 a farmer was driving towards Leicester to sell his eggs, butter, some chickens, and a pig or two. He was approaching a railroad crossing at just the time a train was coming. The driver had been blowing his little horn, but of course the farmer had not been able to hear it over the rattle of the cart and the clucking of the chickens. He saw the train in time to jump. The eggs couldn't jump out of the way so they were scrambled. The chickens and pigs and the horse which was drawing the cart were all killed. Everything was a mess.

The owners of the railroad had not had much concern for this problem until the farmer went to court about his loss. The railroad had to pay for everything, and it cost a lot of money. This made them think.

Mr. Ashten Bagster, the director of the railroad, went to Mr. George Stephenson, who had designed and constructed the "Rocket," and asked him to do something. Mr. Stephenson had no ready solution, and it was Mr. Bagster who finally came up with the proper one. He asked, "If steam pushes the engine, can't it be made to blow a horn loud enough for people to hear for miles?"

Mr. Stephenson contacted a man who made musical instruments, and together they designed a whistle. A steam line was run directly from the boiler to this whistle, and when the steam was released the whistle gave a loud screech.

Isn't it a shame that eight dozen eggs had to be broken, some chickens, a couple of pigs, and a horse killed, and the railroad pay a lot of money before the owners acted as they should have in the first place?

TWO BIRDS

One of the most interesting experiences you can have is visiting Busch Gardens in Tampa, Florida, where there are hundreds of birds. Some of them are large, some are very small. Some have brightly colored feathers, while others are quite drab. Some sing beautiful songs and others simply make funny noises. Some can speak words, others cannot.

On a perch near a walk sat a black myna bird. A boy was standing in front of the bird saying over and over: "Speak to me! Speak to me!" Suddenly the myna bird cocked his head and replied: "Birds don't talk!" Everyone standing near began to laugh, much to the discomfort of the little boy.

Many people have pet birds—we're no exception, we have two. One of ours is a mockingbird. Each morning and evening he comes and perches on the top of our chimney, right above the fireplace in our living room. Here he sits and sings, as if to say good morning as the sun rises or good night as the sun goes to bed. His song is beautiful and varied. Sometimes as we listen to him he sounds like a canary, then again like a lark, or occasionally even like a nightingale. One morning he stopped singing suddenly and I thought he had flown away, then he began to call like a whippoorwill.

That little bird who sits on our chimney is a happy little bird; he must be, or he wouldn't sing so sweetly. But why shouldn't he be happy? He is as free as the wind and can go and come as he likes. He does, however, have to work for his food. On sunny days he can fly from tree to tree and enjoy playing in the grass, as I've sometimes seen him doing. But when he wants something to eat, he must search and dig for it.

Our other bird is in a cage in the kitchen. He's hardly ever allowed out—but he too is happy. He chatters all day long. Now and again he will say, "Pretty Perry, pretty bird." And he is, he's very pretty. His blue feathers are sleek and shiny. No, he can't get out of his cage, he's not free to do as he likes, but he is happy, as happy as his little cousin the mockingbird.

He's happy because he can't have his freedom, because he is confined. He knows that every day he is going to have a cup of fresh seeds and new gravel and some special little treat. He and his cage are kept clean. There is always fresh water provided for him to drink and for his bath. No, he doesn't have his freedom, but he doesn't go hungry either. He never has to sit out for hours in the cold rain. He doesn't have to shiver in the winter or swelter in the summer. In fact, if he did sometime fly from his cage and go out into the wild, he would probably starve—he wouldn't know how to care for himself.

Here are two little birds living under entirely different circumstances and conditions, but both of them are happy. Each finds in his situation something that is worth being happy about, and each one sings lustily to show his appreciation.

TRUSTING
IN THE ARM

In Detroit, Michigan, there is a church located about a mile from the Schaeffer Police Station in a residential area. Like residential sections in many cities, it is quite dark at night. But those of us who belonged to this church were never much concerned about bad boys or girls entering the building and destroying things or taking things that did not belong to them, as some boys or girls do.

Each night, at least twice, a squad car would drive up in front of the church, then around to the back. The two policemen would get out of the automobile and first try the back door, walk to the east door, around to the front, and finally they would see if by any chance the west doors had been left open. Sometimes they found they had. Groups of men or women or of boys or girls might have been meeting in the building during the evening hours and gone away, forgetting to lock one of these many doors.

Immediately after finding a door open, the policemen

would enter the building and go downstairs where they knew there was a telephone and call the minister. It made no difference what time of night it was, and several times he was gotten out of bed to walk two blocks through the snow to the church. They would turn on all the lights in the building, and together would go from room to room to see if any damage had been done, or if anyone was still in the building.

At times the minister had to admit that this was a nuisance, but it was also very gratifying. Everyone in the neighborhood knew of this nightly checkup and knew, too, that there was no set time at which Sergeant Gill or some of his men would arrive. Only once during several years did anyone enter and steal.

We used to say that we put our trust in the "strong arm of the law." There were policemen who were members of the church, but none of them were located at the Schaeffer Station. But that didn't make any difference in the attention that was given our building. We could depend upon the strong arm of the law.

In the book of Psalms we read: "Nor did their own arm give them victory: but thy right hand, and thy arm." "His right hand and his holy arm have gotten him victory." There are many other places in the Bible where we read similar words. The prophet Isaiah once wrote: "He shall gather the lambs with his arm." This sounds comforting; but the great strong arm of God, which protects us and guides us, can also give us a spanking when we need it.

____THE PIG'S BROTHER____

There was once upon a time a little boy, but this little boy was very different from you boys and girls: he never liked to wash his face or hands or take a bath. Sometimes he was so dirty he looked as if the dirt would crack when he moved. His mother tried to get him to keep clean; his father tried to get him to use some soap and water; but no one seemed to be able to do anything with him. Sometimes, I am sorry to say, he would smell bad.

Summer came, and with it vacation time from school. This little boy lived out in the country on a farm, and he had looked forward to the last day of school when he could play with some of the children who lived nearby. But the neighbor children wouldn't play with him. At first he didn't care, there were so many other things he could do. The sun was warm and nice. He could lie in it and watch the leaves of the trees or the clouds being pushed by the wind.

This sermon is not original but is a story often told by the late Dr. Charles N. Arbuckle (Uncle Charlie to his students), Professor at Andover Newton Theological School, as an illustration in story telling. I have never been able to find it in print. He would tell the story and burst into laughter.

After a little while this became very boring, and he wanted someone with whom he could play, someone to talk to. But none of the other children would have anything to do with him. This made him angry and he said to himself, "Who cares, I'll find someone to play with me." So he started to seek a companion.

He went down the road until he saw a little bird sitting on a barbed wire fence. The little boy went up to the bird and said, "Will you play with me?" The little bird looked at the boy and turned away and started to spread his feathers and clean them.

The little boy was not particularly upset. He walked on down the road. In a short time he saw a little kitten who was playing with a flower that was bending over, as if it were begging to be petted by the kitten's paws. "Will you play with me?" asked the little boy. He started to walk toward him, but as he came near, the kitten wrinkled up his nose, turned away, and began to wash himself.

The little boy was now beginning to get upset. Over in a field he saw a horse he was sure would play with him. However he was a bit worried because the horse was so big. The little boy called out, "Mr. Horse, I want someone to play with. Will you play with me? We could run and jump and have lots of fun." The horse trotted over to the little boy, put down his head, and sniffed. He turned his upper lip back from his teeth and galloped a short distance until he found some lovely clean grass, where he lay down and rolled over and over.

It was not long after this that the little boy found a pig wallowing in some mud. The pig was dirty from head to foot. He had a very bad odor, and the little boy almost held his nose. The pig spied the little boy, smiled, and before the little boy could say a word the pig shouted, "Hi, brother, come on over and play!"

SHADOWS

Robert Louis Stevenson wrote a little poem which he called: "My Shadow." He starts it: "I have a little shadow that goes in and out with me." We all cast shadows, have shadows.

There are three words in English that come directly from the Greek language, three words which I expect none of you ever heard: sciagraphy, sciamachy, sciatheric.

Sciagraphy is the art of reading a shadow properly. From where does the shadow come, what causes it and just what does it mean? The best example I can give is when the specialized person takes an x-ray plate and interprets it. This x-ray picture, as we call it, is nothing more than shadows caught on sensitized film when the x-rays pass through a substance, our bodies, a bit of wood, or metal. By understanding these shadows properly, this trained individual can tell many things. In our bodies he can recognize disease from the shadows that are cast.

Our deeds, our behavior are like shadows and tell others much about ourselves. There is an old saying that contains much worth: "Actions speak louder than words."

Pictures are now being taken of the moon and of planets. Shadows in these pictures are most important because from them scientists can determine heights and distances. Events recorded by history are but shadows of something that has taken place. That which has taken place, however, has happened; it cannot be repeated. But from looking at the shadow which is cast, the influence of the event can be considered.

The word "skia" means shadow, and the word "graph" means to trace; put together, they mean to describe a shadow.

The second word we shall think about is "sciamachy." We know the meaning of "skia," now what about the second part of the word? That is "mache" and means a battle. There is such a human habit: boys, girls, mothers, and fathers fight with shadows. They become afraid, upset and concerned about something that has no substance or reality. We are fearful that a shadow might hurt us in some way. Imagination is a good thing when it is used to picture beautiful things in the mind's eye, but when imagination builds up things that don't exist and creates fear, then it becomes truly horrible. We have a term "shadowboxing." In this sort of practice a boxer fights with his own shadow. There is nothing there he can hit, nothing that has weight, and he knows it. Also, the shadow can't strike back at him. Shadowboxing may develop an offensive technique, but it does nothing to help the boxer defend himself. This he must learn in some other way. Fear of a shadow, of something that is nothing, is rather foolish. This is worry. Franklin Delano Roosevelt said in his first inaugural address: "The only thing we have to fear is fear itself."

The last word I would have you think about is "sciatheric." This also is made up of two Greek words: "skia" for shadow and "thera" which means to cure. This word refers to using the shadow constructively. On a sun dial, an upright is fixed so that it will cast a controlled shadow, which will indicate the movement of the sun. Lines are so drawn that when the shadow falls upon them the time of day is indicated. This is a good use for shadows that was discovered many years ago. The prophet Isaiah some seven hundred years before the birth of Jesus wrote: "Behold, I will bring again the shadow of the degrees, which is gone down in the sun dial of Ahaz, ten degrees backward." We know too that the Egyptians used sun dials. Some of the earliest examples of them are to be found in the Berlin museum.

Distinguish between that which is real and that which is shadow. Don't be afraid of that which is nonexistent. Try also to learn what is or has been responsible for a shadow.

DREAMING

You dream, I dream, we all dream. Dreaming is one of the most interesting experiences, and it is something with which we are all familiar. There have been many theories about dreams, and scientists for many years have been trying to learn what takes place during dreams.

It was thought for a long time that dreams were of very short duration, but through the use of electronic equipment, which permits the measuring of the heartbeat and blood pressure, and of small cylinders pressed against the dreamer's throat which record the vibrations of the vocal apparatus during dreaming, much more has been learned.

It seems that our dreams come at regular intervals of about ninety minutes. Dreams are good for us, even when we have nightmares, which sometimes are very upsetting. Some people think we can use our dreams, not only to give relaxation but also to create. It is quite possible that some men like Robert Louis Stevenson let dreams work for them. A Pennsylvania archaeologist in his study of ancient people dreamed the key to read some old writing called Assyrian cuneiform. Dr. Otto Loewi dreamed the theory that helped doctors understand how our nerves work.

The Bible is full of stories of men and women who dreamed. One Bible writer said: "Your old men shall dream dreams, and your young men shall see visions." Many people whose story is told in the Bible thought that God spoke to them in dreams. Who is to say he doesn't?

Often in the Bible we read about an angel appearing to a person in a dream. Perhaps the most famous dream is the one recorded about Jacob, who dreamed that a ladder stretched from earth to heaven with angels going up and down. God stood at the top and said to Jacob: "I am the Lord, the God of Abraham your father and the God of Isaac; the land on which you lie I will give to you and to your descendants." Sarah Adams wrote a hymn telling the story of this dream. Turn to this hymn called "Nearer My God to Thee." Begin reading with the second stanza rather than the first, and you will read about Jacob and how he built an altar to God, then how the ladder appeared. In this hymn Sarah Adams wrote: "There let a way appear, steps unto heaven." It really is a very joyful hymn and should be sung quickly and happily.

Some people are afraid of dreams. This is a shame. We should all welcome and enjoy dreams. Then we too might see God and hear him speak, directing us to a better way of life.

~~~~~~POTATO CHIPS~~~~~~

The story of the creation of potato chips is a fascinating one. During the nineteenth century Saratoga, New York, was a very popular vacation spot. People went there from all parts of the country. The hotels had good dining rooms and there were some famous restaurants. Many of the country's best chefs were employed in the town.

A particular customer at the Moon's Lake House seemed to be constantly grumbling. One of the things about which he complained the most was the french fries served at the hotel. Each meal he would send word to the chef, through his waiter, that the french fries were soggy, limp, or too greasy. One day, when the complaint was taken back to the kitchen, Chef George Crum responded, "I'll make them crisp enough for him!" He proceeded to slice potatoes very thin, then he dropped them, one by one, into very hot fat. The wafers of potato came out brown, very crisp, and without much grease. They were salted and taken to the fussy guest. The man loved them and began to sing praises to the chef.

Other people in the hotel heard of the remarkable creation

and demanded to try them too. It was not long until "Sara-toga Chips," as they were called, became one of the most popular items on the hotel menu.

How many hundreds of tons of potatoes are prepared in this fashion all over the world today? In the United States and Canada we eat them all the time. Some people buy them in pound packages, others in five- or ten-pound drums, and many others purchase them in little bags.

Potato chips can sometimes be very bad. If they are left exposed to the air, they become limp and are not good at all. If they are stale, the fat becomes rancid and they taste terrible.

Does it sound silly to think we people are like potato chips? Sometimes you and I are alert, snappy, and sharp. At other times we are just like wet chips, bad and sour, annoying everyone who comes in contact with us.

There are some chips you want to get rid of as quickly as possible after you bite them. So it is with people. When we are disagreeable, people want to get rid of us as soon as possible.

If potato chips are to be good, they must be given proper care. When they come from the factory they are in airtight bags. If we want people to like us we must give ourselves proper care too. We must think good thoughts, do kind things, keep our eyes open for need, and do all we can to help correct wrong situations.

Much as we might wish to blame others for the kind of person we are, we cannot. We are our own responsibility.

DUST

In Birmingham, Alabama, a gentleman named Mr. Dimick owns and operates a large foundry. It is a fascinating place to visit. The blast furnaces roar; the white-hot metal splashes. The melted iron is poured into sand molds. The castings are removed, ground down, and polished.

One day while visiting this gentleman in this big factory, we walked into the repair shop and had to step aside as one of the workmen drove a large "end loader" into the shop. An "end loader" is a tractor with a big scoop on the front of it which enables one man to pick up, lift, and, if necessary, carry a lot of dirt at a time. In the foundry these end loaders are used for transporting sand from one place to another.

The workman got down from the seat of the tractor and picked up an insulated hose which led to a powerful steam boiler. He pressed the valve at the end of the hose and allowed the live steam to escape in a jet. With this steam he cleaned each joint on the machine very carefully. Noticing my interest Mr. Dimick said, "Yes, this is done all the time; it must be, for these machines cost a lot of money and they simply can't take the dust; it eats them to bits." He continued, "We must change the air filters on these motors three to four times a day. They are not like the human body. People breathe this dust day in and day out; I've been breathing it for thirty years, but an engine couldn't breathe it for more than a few days before it would be completely ruined."

What is the difference between a man and a machine? God made man and man made the machine. That's the whole difference! Man is very clever and is constantly refining his product, inventing ways of protecting it, like with air filters and proper oil. God has refined the human body so that it can stand much abuse. We must almost deliberately try to destroy ourselves.

It has been said that the body is the temple of the Lord. It is a sacred trust. Yet many people have no respect for their bodies. Newspapers are constantly calling to our attention how we introduce, deliberately, harmful substances into our bodies, almost as if trying to see just how much they can take and still continue to function. The Cancer Society and the Food and Drug Administration inform us of the harmfulness of cigarettes; warnings are even now printed on each package, yet we continue to smoke. Everyone knows that drugs such as alcohol and morphine are harmful, yet we insist on putting these substances into our bodies.

A long time ago the apostle Paul said: "Do you not know that your body is a temple of the Holy Spirit?" And in his letter to the Ephesians he wrote: "There is one body, and one spirit." Our bodies are a sacred trust from God, and surely it is our duty to care for them.

LIGHTS

Looking down on a great city at night from the top of a tall building or from an airplane is thrilling. There are thousands of lights—bright, dim, green, blue, white, red, yellow, gold. Some of these lights represent illuminated signs which speak of industry or of the efforts of men to find pleasure.

There are clusters of lights which represent great factories or hospitals. These lights tell many stories. Those coming from the factories speak of work; those from the hospital windows speak of pain, suffering, worry, fear, anxiety, or great joy. They speak of birth, life, and death.

There are many scattered little lights that mark our homes, the houses such as those in which you and I live. These lights tell of boys, girls, and their mothers and fathers. Some of these lights are in happy homes; some of them shine forth from sad and broken homes.

In the center of the city of Boston is the State House dome. When you see it lighted you remember the history of this nation of ours and the laws which govern the actions of the people of Massachusetts. There are two kinds of lights which you see: direct and indirect, or reflected. There is the light that comes from the great floodlights and the light that is reflected from the gold leaf on the dome. Often it is difficult to distinguish between the real and the sham. Some men are like the great lights themselves, others are but reflections of the glory of another. Jesus once said: "If then the light in you is darkness, how great is the darkness."

There were few or no street lights in London during the reign of Queen Anne in the eighteenth century. With her approval a law was passed; everyone paying ten pounds rent, whose property fronted on a street or alley, was required to hang out a light during the hours from six to eleven in the evening during the months from September till March. It was declared that everyone was responsible for the safety of his neighbors from the dangers of the night. A warder with a lanthorn (a lantern) and a halberd (a kind of long-handled weapon with a spear and ax combined) went about the streets crying: "Hang out your lights." Paul wrote to the Ephesians, "For once you were darkness, but now you are light in the Lord; walk as children of light."

A man may become a truly bad man if he has no help or is given no direction. It was the watchman's task in London to go around to all the houses at dusk, beating on the doors and ringing his bell to warn people that it was time to hang out their lights. It is just as much our job, today, to show people the way to Christ and warn them that now is the time to do something about making their lives better.

PAIN

There are various kinds of pain—physical, mental, emotional, social, and even spiritual. Medical doctors have discovered many types of substances which will deaden physical aches. Some people resort to drugs of various kinds to quiet emotional discomfort.

What is the purpose of pain? This is a question often asked. The answer is very simple: to give warning that there is something wrong. There are people who have what is called a very high tolerance of pain. If such a person developed appendicitis, he might not notice the pain and his appendix might rupture.

Sometimes pain is persistent; it becomes what we call chronic. We may let this condition damage us or we can learn to utilize our pain. We can accept it as a stimulant to do great things.

Pearls are very beautiful. Like many beautiful things they come directly as the result of pain. Some irritating substance, a bit of sand or perhaps a small worm, gets inside the oyster shell and bothers the oyster. The substance cannot be dislodged so the oyster surrounds the foreign matter with juice that hardens, forming a smooth, lustrous surface over the irritating bit of matter so that it no longer hurts.

Both diamonds and coal are carbon. But you wouldn't want to wear a bit of coal mounted on a ring, so they are not actually the same, are they? Then what makes the diamond more acceptable, more beautiful? The diamond has been subjected to very intense heat and tremendous pressure.

When gold or iron or copper is in its natural state, it is of little or no use to us. The ore must be crushed and subjected to great heat first. We call this process refinement.

Beautiful, wonderful characters are formed in the same manner. They must be subjected to the process of refinement. There is an old saying: "The mills of God grind slowly, but they grind exceedingly small." This is a way of saying almost the same thing.

You and I don't like pain; we do all we can to avoid it. If the oyster remains undisturbed it will not produce a pearl. If people are not disturbed they will do nothing about their characters. Not all people know how to turn their hurts to advantages. Some crumble under the heat and pressure of misfortune instead of becoming diamonds or rubies, or creating pearls of great price.

Many of the finest people I have known have had trouble, some of them very great trouble. Instead of becoming peevish and sour under pain and suffering, they have grown more saintly and wonderful.

____MAKING UP NAMES____

Ever since the founding of the colonies, lumbering has been one of the very important industries of the United States. Millions of board feet, tons of lumber, have been cut every year. For many years we have been so careless of this precious heritage that we have now almost finished cutting all the virgin timber which has been growing in God's garden for hundreds of years.

Some states have become more conscious of the need to protect their lumber. In places like Alabama, where lumbering is one of the most important sources of wealth, tree farms have been developed. Trees are properly planted and fed, and no one is permitted to cut a tree until it has grown to prescribed proportions. When one tree is cut, another must be planted to take its place. If this were not done, it is quite possible that your children might not have any lumber at all.

Lumber is used for making houses, for furniture, for cutting blocks in kitchens. Some of it is even used as it was years ago for making bowls and plates. It is thought the height of fashion to be able to use such wooden bowls in setting a table. Beautiful lamps are also made from wood.

The men who harvest lumber were named, and are still called, "lumberjacks." The word "jack" once referred to a kind of leather coat which was worn by many men for protection, not only in battle but also to keep their bodies from being scratched when they walked or worked in the forests. Because of this common use it later became a name describing a common man. Lumberjacks then were men who cut and hauled lumber. Steeplejacks were men who climbed and worked on steeples and in high places.

Workers in lumber camps made up special names for various things. They called griddle cakes or pancakes "flats." Instead of asking for a stack of cakes as people would today, they called for a string of flats. A bad cook was known as a "sizzler," and an assistant cook in the lumber camp was a "flunkie."

Owners of lumber camps found it was not profitable to let the men return to camp for lunch because they would take too much time from their work, so food was taken to them in the woods. This food was scornfully called "nosebag shows."

Most of these names didn't hurt anyone. But the terms "sizzler" and "flunkie" were uncomplimentary and cruel.

Have you noticed when there is someone we don't like we make up names to describe him? This is a very bad habit, one which most of us need to overcome. Some unthinking people speak of Italians as "wops" or "dagos," Jews as "kikes," and Negroes as "niggers." This is not a good practice because it hurts the people who are called by these names.

A few years ago when someone did not like another he would say, "You're an I.W.W.," or a "Bolshi." Today everyone who does not think just as we think, or does not believe everything we believe, or is a little different from what we are, is apt to be called a "Commie" or a "Red." Often the person using the term and the person called the name do not know the basis on which communism has been built, or what the name really means. This then is dishonest, both for the person who uses the name and the person to whom it is given.

Boys and girls, mothers and fathers, need to learn to guard their tongues and call things by their proper and right names if the made-up new names might be harmful and cruel.

TOO MUCH?

The dictionary tells us that the word "affluent" means flowing abundantly, well supplied with material things. More simply it means being rich.

We live in what is called an "affluent society." It is true many people in the United States do not have as much as others in the way of material things. But it is also a recognized fact that the people of this country have far more than any other people have ever had. Most of us have nice homes and too much to eat. To a student of history it seems strange that people should have too much to eat, and that being fat is a danger to many people's lives. Sometimes it is said that folks eat themselves into their graves.

This can do strange things to our thinking. We are apt to take too much for granted and may become lazy. Many young people starting married life expect to have right then just as much as their parents do after twenty-five or thirty years of homemaking. They expect to have everything without working for it. We have so many automobiles that many are completely shocked at the thought of walking a couple of blocks.

It is a very good thing for us to think about the men and

61

women who settled this land and of the effort and hardship they had to suffer. Through hardship they became strong and resilient. Even after the settlers of New England had learned how to eat corn and were growing rye, and after they had learned to fish, there always came the "six weeks' want" each spring when the vegetables in the root celler were wilted and mildewed. Then what a thrill it was when the milkweed began to grow and there was marsh marigold and nettle to be harvested and put into the stew pot.

Women churned butter by hand and prepared what food they could get in order that their menfolks would have enough strength to clear the land and build stone walls. All of this sounds very harsh to us because there are very few of us who have ever known anything like it.

There are two references in the New Testament I'd like you to remember. Maybe you've heard them before, or maybe they are completely new to you. Dr. Luke, in the beginning of the book of the Acts of the Apostles, tells of the ascension of the spirit of Christ into heaven. "He was lifted up, and a cloud took him out of their sights." But it is what follows that can be of very great importance to you. A man in white appeared to the disciples and said, "Men of Galilee, why do you stand looking into heaven?" Or in other words, it was as if the man said, "You had it good while Jesus was here, he told what to do and think. Now he's not here—get going; he taught you how and what to do. Get busy; nothing can be accomplished by just standing and dreaming."

The other is a quotation from Paul's letter to the Romans. In the twelfth chapter he wrote: "Never flag in zeal, be aglow with the Spirit, serve the Lord, . . . contribute to the needs of the saints, practice hospitality."

There is much work to be done; there is much to be learned. If you put your heart to it, you'll find that it's more fun than doing nothing or having everything handed to you.

PEDDLERS

It must have been such fun in the early days of our country when the peddler came to the door. After people became settled into an area they began to have wants beyond their needs. The first peddlers came carrying their wares on their backs. Later they had horse-drawn carts. What a host of things they had for sale: coffee roasters, coffee mills, jelly molds, cherry pitters, apple corers, lemon squeezers, needles and thread, bolts of cloth, brooms, tea, white sugar, baking tins, candlesticks, and many others.

We have so many labor-saving devices in our homes today that you children and many adults just take for granted, but a few years ago there were none of these. There are many things which add to our pleasure and comfort, not really essential, but we think they are necessary. If men and women of seventy-five years ago could step into one of our homes today, they would be simply lost amidst the variety of things. They wouldn't know how to turn on the lights; they'd have no idea what an electric dishwasher was or how it worked. Air conditioning would be to them the eighth wonder of the world.

Today we go into a supermarket and pick up dozens of things that would have been completely unknown a hundred years ago. Frozen things, for example, would appear ridiculous. Even just a few years ago when milk, delivered at the side door, became frozen on a cold winter night the housewife considered it spoiled and would not dare give it to her family. Meat, vegetables, or any food that was accidentally frozen was thrown away.

What a different world we live in today. Yet how much is the same. Why the same? Because the world of today, just like the world of yesterday, is populated by men, women, boys, and girls who think and behave just as men, women, boys, and girls did a hundred years, five hundred years, a thousand, and ten thousand years ago. We love, hate, admire, distrust just as people have been doing over the centuries.

Some would tell us that the teachings of Jesus are old-fashioned, out of date, simply because they were given to men two thousand years ago. To say this is foolish, because men are good, bad, and indifferent now, just as they were then. Too, the things that we really need are the same today as they always have been. We need to be clean, have somewhere comfortable to sleep, have something to eat, and someone to love us. So, the things that Jesus said have just the same meaning as they did when he spoke to the people two thousand years ago. They mean as much now as two hundred years ago when the peddler came with his horse and cart and his load of goods.

LET'S HAVE
A TREAT

There are many kinds of treats we can enjoy. It can be a treat to go to a motion-picture show, to attend the circus, to walk in the woods, to play with a friend, to have something good to eat which we haven't had for a long time. One of the meanings of the word "treat" is to give oneself or another something that is particularly gratifying.

The Pennsylvania Dutch are known for their good things to eat. These are people who came from Germany, Holland, and Switzerland and brought with them their "old country" favorites in foods. But when they settled in this country they found new and varied ways of treating things which grew in abundance here.

When we hear about the wonderful meals that were prepared day after day we wonder how there could possibly be things that were food treats, but there were.

At Easter time the Pennsylvania Dutch mother would spend many hours and days in preparation—cracking nuts, grating chocolate, baking cookies by the bushel so that there would be enough for anyone who happened to visit the house during the holiday. For weeks the kitchen would smell of good things, and when the weather was warm enough to have the doors and windows open, the odor would drift out across the fields where the men and children would be working.

It was difficult to color Easter eggs in those days. It was hard to find substances that would dye the shell without doing harm to the interior or poisoning the boys and girls. Beet juice was excellent for turning eggs red. Other colors were not so easy to come by. A few people knew that if wax were applied to the eggshell, color would not stick and designs could be made in this way. Pennsylvania mothers would take the point of a sharp knife and with it scrape off the dye to draw pictures. Boys and girls and, I expect, mothers and fathers looked forward to these wonderful treats—something different or something particularly nice.

Some things that you consider a treat others would not. I had a friend who was born and raised in central Africa. One of the treats he missed when he came to live in the United States was chunky white grubworms fried in deep fat. I don't think that would be a treat for most of you; it certainly wouldn't for me. But he considered it so and many times expressed the wish that he might have some.

The Bible is filled with treats. There are stories of adventure and stories of exploration. There are love stories. Gideon, Deborah, Esther, Paul, Ruth contribute some wonderful treats. There are many stories of destruction, but there are also great stories of construction, the building of great cities or temples.

The special treats of the Bible are the stories about Jesus and his friends. Once a group of boys and girls wanted to talk to him. The disciples were interested in what the Master was saying to them and told the youngsters to go away. Jesus said to them: "Let the children come to me." He then played with them, told them stories, explained to them how they could be more happy, and did so in language that they understood. He gave them many treats.

~~~~SOURDOUGH~~~~

Did you ever try to count the various kinds of crackers and bread on sale in the supermarket? There are big crackers, small crackers, round ones, square ones. Some are cut in diamond shapes, others in the form of animals.

It seems too that every month there is a new cereal introduced. Each one of them is supposed to have a finer flavor than any other and to be more nutritious, if we are to believe the advertisers. Most of these breads, crackers, and cereals are made from grains—wheat, corn, barley, oats, or often combinations of them.

These mixtures of flavors of basic grains are everyday items in the diet of most Americans, but this was not so until just recently. Not long ago people wouldn't have known what to do with these manufactured foods. Nor would they have enjoyed many of those things we use for food. Mark Twain once said that "tasters are made, not born." This has become a motto of the American advertising man, and he spends much of his life conditioning us to eat and drink everything that will help increase consumption and make money.

A few years ago the basic food in the diet of many people, particularly the cowboys and miners of the west, was a bread called "sourdough." Really, however, this is one of the oldest kinds of bread known to man. We know this method of preparing bread was used back as far as four thousand years before the birth of Jesus. But it is believed that sourdough was unknown in the Americas until Columbus came, carrying sourdough starter in his ship.

Yeast is the name we use for a group of very small plants which have the ability to change sugar into alcohol and carbon dioxide. We all know and like the bubbles in soft drinks. When yeast works in a mixture of flour and water it produces similar bubbles. This creates small or large holes in the dough and makes it what we call light and edible. Today your mother may buy yeast in the store in little square cakes or packages of dried particles. She simply adds a little warm sugar water and it begins to work. But it was not always this easy. For thousands of years yeast would settle on or in dough accidentally. When this happened, after making bread, the cook or housewife would carefully save a little raw dough. Sometimes the cook out on the western plains or in Alaska would take his "starter" to bed with him on cold nights so that it would remain warm and be ready and "working" the next day for flapjacks and bread.

The apostle Paul, writing to the people of Corinth said, "Do you not know that a little leaven ferments the whole lump of dough?" What he was suggesting to the Corinthians and to us is that we must watch our behavior and actions, because, even though we may not be aware of it, every moment of our lives we are having an influence on other people. If we smile, people will smile back. If we are mean, others will act mean toward us. If we love, people will love us; they can't help themselves.

Try an experiment. Think of someone you know who doesn't like you. Love this person with all your might. At first they will pay no attention to you. Keep on loving them. Let nothing they say or do bother you or make you change from loving them. It may take a long time, but eventually they will start loving you in return. Best of all, you'll have a lot of fun watching the change that will take place.

CASTLES

Today castles are of little value as protection, yet for many hundreds of years men depended upon fortresses and walls to keep them safe from harm. The lord of an area would construct his central building, "the keep." Around this he built the living quarters for his retainers: the bakery, the tailor's shop, the armory, the stables, and other necessary places.

The castles were massive, with walls sometimes several feet thick. They were very high. As you look at one of them today you wonder at the engineering knowledge necessary for their construction, particularly when you realize that the people of earlier days did not have our modern tools and equipment for moving heavy loads. Some castles were located on the top of hills, some even on mountains, giving them command of a large area. Others were on peninsulas extending out into the sea or a lake. Locations were chosen with an eye to using as much natural protection as possible, assuring greatest control of a district.

Although grim, some castles are very beautiful. The alcazar at Segovia, built by Henry IV of Castile, took a period of twenty-five years to construct, beginning in 1454. Perhaps the most beautiful of all is the castle of Neuschwanstein in Bavaria.

Two of the greatest castles of Great Britain are Caernarvon Castle in Wales, begun in 1283, and Windsor, which is on a spot that has been fortified from the eleventh century. The Kremlin in Moscow is also an ancient castle.

Those castles which did not have natural protection of the sea, a lake, or a river were usually surrounded by a moat. It is very interesting to visit the Tower of London, which has the river on one side and on the other three a deep ditch which used to be kept filled with water.

All fortified castles have certain things in common—thick walls, towers which permitted sentries to look in all directions watching for attack, slots in the walls from which arrows could be shot. There were very few entrances to castles. In many cases it was most difficult to get into a castle except by the one main gate.

Living is like this. Men have discovered that to enter into a good life one must follow the teachings of Jesus.

There is another analogy. It is difficult for the spirit of Jesus to enter our hearts. We build up walls around ourselves, shutting out everything. We build these walls for protection, but they become instead prison walls through which we seem unable to escape. There are gates, however, into our lives which we can open to admit the spirit of Christ. The psalmist sang: "Lift up your heads, O ye gates! and be lifted up, O ancient doors! that the King of glory may come in." "Open to me the gates of righteousness."

The ancient castles had what was called a portcullis, a grating of wood or iron which slipped down to guard the gate. The psalmist suggests we must open the gate to our hearts, must draw up the portcullis, in order that the love of God can get in. No one can do this for us; we must do it for ourselves.

A WHITEWASHED WALL

We've all enjoyed Mark Twain's story of how the boys were persuaded to help whitewash a wall. It is easy to make us do something we really don't want to do by glamorizing it. The apostle Paul suggested that Satan acts with many kinds of forces. Once he wrote to some of his friends that he would like to have visited them, but Satan prohibited him. I think Paul was perfectly sincere in this. Something or someone was constantly interfering with what he knew he should do. He found himself doing what he wanted to do rather than what he should have done.

There is a wonderful story in the twenty-third chapter of the book of Acts. Paul had returned to Jerusalem and was arrested. After he had claimed Roman citizenship he was released. Then those who hated him were able to trump up charges sufficient to have him brought before the council of the high priest. He had begun his defense when Ananias, the high priest, commanded that Paul be struck on the mouth.

Paul was angry at this unjust treatment and said to the high priest, "God shall strike you, you whitewashed wall!"

Why do people whitewash a wall, or paint one? The answer is very simple: because it is dirty. Paul was attempting to point out to the high priest that before attempting to destroy a man's character he should look at his own.

It's very easy to say what is wrong with the other fellow. Jesus referred to this same bad habit when he suggested that we look for the beam in our own eye before we become concerned about the sliver in the eye of someone else.

We recognize that all men have faults. My mother used to often quote an old saying which I am sure you have heard: "Everyone is queer except me and thee, and sometimes I almost think that thou art."

Much better than trying to cover something up is eliminating it, to get rid of it. Chlorine bleach is for the purpose of getting stain out of clothing. Soap is for the purpose of washing away that which is dirty. If a boy has a dirty face, you don't paint over the dirt; the best thing is to use some warm water, a washcloth, and some soap.

If you have a dirty character you should clean it up. The washcloth is the church, and the soap is the love of the spirit of Christ. These two used properly will bring about some wonderful results. Some boys and girls think they can get along without these two things, with the result that we have some rather dirty boys and girls. Often they realize they are dirty and try to cover up. As paint does rather a good job of hiding, so a sweet smile, a kind word not really meant, a false consideration for others can hide what we really are.

You know what kind of a character you have. You must correct the situation, not cover it up.

Don't be a whitewashed wall; some day a rainstorm may come and sweep away the whitewash, and everyone will see your true color.

A MUSIC BOX

After a visit to Europe a high school girl brought back home several lovely keepsakes. Perhaps her prized possession is a music box from Switzerland. It is in the form of a small Swiss chalet with animals in the front yard. When the hinged roof is lifted beautiful music begins to play. There is a mountain in the background and in the foreground, a mountain climber with his alpine horn.

During the eighteenth century snuff boxes were very popular. Snuff is pulverized tobacco, which today is held in the mouth but then was forcibly inhaled through the nose. Dandies of the past liked to call attention to themselves just as we do today. Their snuff boxes were extremely beautiful and often contained music boxes, so that not only the beauty of the box and the sneeze which followed the use of the snuff, but also the pretty sound would draw people's attention.

The sound of music is produced by two things hidden inside the box. One is a flat piece of steel resembling a comb. The teeth of this comblike object are cut at different lengths so that each has a different vibration and gives off a particular sound. The second thing is a brass cylinder studded with pins which is slowly revolved by a spring mechanism. As these cleverly placed pins pluck the teeth in the correct sequence, they produce a melody. The little machine which moves the cylinder is very like one which works a clock. Some of the workmanship which goes into a music box is very special and can be done only by highly trained experts.

Music boxes come in many forms and many sizes. You may have seen musical jewelry boxes or powder boxes on your mother's dressing table. There are some boxes as large as picnic baskets or bedroom chests which play a number of tunes one after another. Then there are some music boxes which are so small you wonder at the hand which crafted them and the mind which conceived them. Music boxes have been built into things which the owner does not want moved. The moment this object, a bottle or a box, is picked up or its position changed, it begins to play. Music boxes have been built into alarm clocks so that a merry tune rather than a harsh bell awakes the sleeper.

A music box has a spring to drive its mechanism. So, too, all of us must have something within ourselves to drive us. S. S. Curry, a famous speech teacher, used to tell his students: "What you say must come from within outward." What he meant was that unless you are completely sincere in what you say, it is better to keep your mouth shut. To be effective, what you say must be honest and come from the heart.

A further lesson from the music box is that everything we say or do should be lovely, appealing, or of some worth. There is enough in our world that is sordid, unhappy, drab, or uninteresting. If we know something to say which is unkind about another person, it is better to keep it to ourselves.

Most people like music boxes and enjoy the sounds which they produce. Most people admire and appreciate the workmanship which goes into the construction of a music box. Wouldn't it be fine if people felt the same way about your character and the things you do or say?

‿‿‿‿NEAR THE HEAT‿‿‿‿‿

We really don't know who invented the barbecue. It is con-
jectured that the name may have come from the French
barbe à queue, which means from beard to tail. But more
probably it is from the Carib: **barbacoa,** which is a sort of
gridiron. The Carib is a tribe of American Indians now main-
ly confined to South America, but originally from the islands
of the Caribbean Sea.

The barbecue as we know it is a way of preparing food,
and the Mexicans are so good at it that we might think it was
they who originated the method. They dig a hole in the
ground, about four feet deep and two feet in diameter. They
plaster mud along the walls to keep them from collapsing.
In the bottom of this pit they put some light, porous stones.
They use a particular kind of stone which holds heat but
will not crack. Over the stones they place enough dry wood
to fill the pit. The wood is then lighted and allowed to burn
until it becomes a bed of hot coals.

Leaves of the maguey plant are wilted over the fire. These
leaves give moisture and flavor to the meat. They are used

to line the pit, the tips of the leaves pointing down toward the coals. On a grate is placed an earthenware pot containing rice, chick peas, potatoes, peppers, and perhaps some other vegetables. The meat is always placed on top of all other things.

The maguey leaves are then folded over the meat to make a kind of cover. This is held in place by a palm-leaf mat, and the hole is then filled up with mud. It takes at least six to eight hours to properly cook everything. After the food has been distributed, the broth is served as a drink.

This is quite different from the way Americans prepare a barbecue in the back yard. We simply take some charcoal, light it, and wait until there is a bed of hot coals, then quickly cook the meat a little, usually using steak or hamburger. Sometimes we'll bake potatoes or corn on the coals, but not often. This takes too much time, and we Americans want everything in a hurry.

We have a large barbecue oven in our back yard. That's the only trouble with it—it's too large. It is beautifully made of red brick and lined with yellow "fire brick." This oven is so very big that it takes a lot of charcoal to get any heat. Then it is difficult to adjust the grate on which the food is placed for cooking; it is far too high above the fire. There must be heat or the meat does not cook. The charcoal must be completely red with a gray ash covering it; otherwise the meat gets too much smoke to be good. The nearness of the fire depends on the thickness of the meat.

In order to get things done in life you must have what grown-ups call incentive. In other words, there must be something to make you want to do things and do them right. Sometimes other people must urge you, your parents or perhaps a teacher. But the best "urger" you can have is a desire within yourself to please God. The spirit of God is like the heat from the fire which properly prepares men so that they may be useful to others. I wouldn't say we've got to be properly barbecued, but it is much the same thing. The heat of God must warm us to just the right degree in order that we may do the things in this world that we should do.

WHAT'S IN A NAME?

Do you enjoy a parade? There are all sorts of parades. Circus parades were once very popular. A circus would come into a town, and as soon as the tents had been set up, the men and women would get into their costumes and mount the circus wagons. Some wagons would carry the animals, others, scenes from some of the side shows. There would always be a steam calliope, a kind of organ with the pipes activated by steam rather than air. Young women, or women who looked young, would ride the elephants while their handlers led them down the street. The clowns in their varied dress would perform tricks to try to get men, women, boys, and girls to laugh.

There are many older men and women who will never forget the circus parade of their younger years and could today in their mind's eye easily line up and watch it again as it passed along the streets of the town in which they were raised.

There have always been military parades. In the ancient days of Rome and Greece they were usually in the form of triumphal marches. Often a particular arch would be constructed in honor of a hero or of a battle, and the returning victorious forces would march beneath it.

Today the parades through Times Square in New York are not unlike those ancient marches. In old Rome flowers would often be thrown into the path of the marchers; today ticker tape is thrown from high windows and goes streaming over the throng.

Each year millions of eyes are fastened upon the television screen as people are fascinated by the "Miss America" and "Miss Universe" contests and the lovely girls as they parade before the judges and the entire nation.

When you grow older and study the works of William Shakespeare, you may read where one of his characters asks, "What's in a name?" A name is only a symbol on a bit of paper that suggests to us how to make the sound. But is that all it is? No, of course not; it suggests you or me. Yet a name is far more than that. It usually stands for a lot of people. It stands for your family.

Have you ever wondered what it would be like if all of your ancestors, starting with your parents, then your grandparents, your great-grandparents and their parents, and so on back for a thousand years, could march in a parade before you? Some of them would be very nice people, you'd like them a lot. But don't forget some of them would be absolute stinkers. Some of them would be men and women of high principles; others would be thieves, robbers, people without ethical standards. Each one of them has given special meaning to your name during his lifetime. When your name has been spoken, what they have been like is the meaning the name has suggested to others.

When others hear the name as it refers to you, how do

they react? Is it a good name in their hearing? Do they thrill when it is spoken? Does the sound of it make them happy? Or, when they hear it, do they scoff, become upset, or do you find they are all disturbed?

I hope that when the name you carry is spoken, people will feel you have carried it with honor, that you have added a little worthwhile glory to it. Will you strive to live so that when the name Brown, Smith, Petosky, or whatever is spoken, others will think: "He is a good boy, girl, man, or woman; I'm glad I have known this person"?

TRAPS

There are all sorts and all sizes of traps. There are big traps, little traps, and middle-sized traps. There are mousetraps, bear traps, lobster traps, flytraps, and traps for big game.

Mousetraps are made in various ways; the most common is simply a board on which has been fastened a piece of wire, activated by a strong spring. A bit of food, generally some cheese, is placed on a delicately balanced trigger, and when the mouse moves the trigger the heavy wire snaps over him and breaks his back.

A bear trap is somewhat the same as a mousetrap, but instead of the wire, strong jaws of steel come together and grab the animal that steps in it. The trap is placed in the path which the animal has often followed. Honey or something else that attracts the animal is placed near by.

Lobster traps are very different in shape. They are constructed with wood lattice. One end of the trap is open and some fish placed inside the box of laths. The open end, however, has a net funnel of cord going into the box so that the lobster can crawl in but not out again. Flytraps are often constructed in the same way, and flys are attracted by some foul-smelling food or a light. They enter but can't get out again. Some of the more modern flytraps electrocute the flies.

Big game hunters in Africa dig holes in the ground, cover them over so that the animal can't see them, and place some food that the animal can smell at the bottom of the hole. Sometimes the hole is kept uncovered and a small animal which the big game would like to eat is placed at the bottom. The tiger, or lion, or whatever it may be, jumps into the hole for the food and can't climb out.

What have all these traps in common? Of course you know —we call it bait, something that will attract whatever is to be caught. There are all sorts of traps for boys and girls, and for men and women, too. Someone would persuade us to do something that is wrong, something dishonest or unkind. We are attracted by wrong being made to appear good and fine. "It's so much fun, you must try it. You don't know what you are missing. Don't be a square. Come on, jump in; the water's fine." These are words which are bait that we all know only too well.

The first few chapters of the book of Genesis contain some wonderful word pictures. First we have pictures of the general way in which the creation and evolution of man must have taken place. There was no attempt on the part of these ancient writers to give scientific explanations. They just painted word pictures of what they imagined took place.

In the third chapter is told the story of a trap. The ancient writer says that a snake spoke to Eve and said to her: "There's some fruit on that tree over there. You've been told that you mustn't eat it because it is poison and if you do you'll die. That's not true; it is sweet and good. It is the finest fruit in all of the land. You can have it and have it now, you don't have to wait for God's permission. He's nowhere around. Come on, I've eaten some, I'm not dead, try it."

Finally, Eve takes the bait and eats of the tree which God had forbidden man to eat. The story ends with punishment. Adam and Eve are driven out of the garden. Now, had they but waited, there's no doubt God would have given permission for them to eat. But they didn't wait. Today we have research. What is research? It is asking God's permission. And when he is ready he gives it, and man learns more about himself, the world in which he lives, and God.

THE POND

In the southern section of New Hampshire, known as the "Lakes Region," are many beautiful lakes, or "ponds" as they are called. There are Lovell, Great East, Pine River, Round, Ossipee, Balch, Province, and the larger lakes: Wentworth and Winnipesaukee. Hundreds and thousands of men, women, and children push their way from New York, Boston, and all over Connecticut and Massachusetts each weekend to visit this area. Other people come from all over America. Most of these folks from Chicago, Minneapolis, Birmingham, Atlanta, and other faraway places own cottages in this section, and they visit them as often as they possibly can.

At least one of these lakes is losing much of its natural beauty. The water level has been going down year after year. Recently many cottages have been built on its shores. The people who have built want the feeling of roughing it with all the modern conveniences as cheaply as possible. All of them have installed inside bathrooms with complete toilet facilities. These have called for water, and more water. The easiest and cheapest way of securing water is simply to install a pump with a pressure tank and run a plastic pipe into the lake.

City folks have long been very wasteful of water. They have gone into this water wonderland and carried with them their wastefulness. This little lake, nestled down between the hills, is completely fed by mountain streams, and with summer residents drawing off so much water there is simply not enough flowing in to meet the demand.

There are a number of lessons here. We are a very wasteful generation. We do not care, it would seem, what there is left of natural resources or natural beauty as long as we have what we want for ourselves and our own convenience.

Some people behave like this with regard to the church. They will take all they can get, never giving anything or caring if there is anything for others. Some people get married, adopting the same philosophy.

Another lesson is personal. You cannot give out unless you take in. There are those who do not read after they have graduated from high school or even college. They say, "We have completed our education." These people are never stimulated to think, and life becomes nothing more than a case of eating and drinking. What they may have acquired in school is soon gone, and with nothing to take its place they become dull.

There must also be an intake of things spiritual to give strength in times of need. In day-to-day living all of us come up against problems, some of them small, but others of large proportions. They can get us down, defeat us, unless we have what is called inner strength. If there is nothing in the depths of our souls, then we can draw nothing.

Jesus said, "Come to me, and I will give."

COPPLE CROWN
MOUNTAIN

In eastern New Hampshire there is a mountain called Copple Crown. Today it is all grown over, but years ago a trail ran up one side, over the top, and down the other. Many people used this road even though climbing was hard; it was shorter by several miles than the one running around the base of the mountain.

One boy named Tim used the trail regularly, for he was courting a girl who lived on the opposite side from his house. Copple Crown has so many caves it is almost completely hollow, so the whole mountain acts as if it were a great drum, exaggerating the sounds of horses' hooves or wagon wheels. Often at night someone would say, "There goes Tim to visit Mary" or "Tim's been seeing Mary tonight and is on his way home." Now Tim didn't realize this. No one had ever mentioned that his mountain rides were known by all those living in the valley.

About once a year Mary's parents went to Portsmouth

for supplies. It was fun for them to visit the big city, but it was a long, hard trip, almost forty miles, so they were gone several days.

On the way back this one time there was some snow, so the trip from Dover north took a little longer than usual. When they finally arrived, they were surprised to find the fire dead and no pot of stew hanging on the crane in the fireplace. Mary was not in the cabin and hadn't left a note to tell them where she had gone. At first they weren't too concerned. No one had ever been molested in those parts; they had no fear of leaving her alone.

The next day when she still had not come home they started to worry and search for her. Not far from the barn they found her body, badly beaten. It looked as if a fiend had beaten her. Who possibly could have done this thing? Tim never entered their minds because they didn't know of their daughter's interest in him. Somehow the young couple had kept their meetings secret from their parents. Not so with the neighbors. Immediately when they learned of the tragedy they blamed him.

The boy was arrested and taken to Dover. He was brought to trial, protesting his innocence. "I didn't even know the girl," he claimed. "Besides, if I did there are no witnesses who could swear that I was there and a man is assumed innocent until he is found guilty."

Then one witness after another took the stand to declare they had heard Tim's horse crossing the mountain on the very night Mary had been murdered. When there were fewer automobiles people could recognize them by their sound. Farmers didn't need to look when a car approached their house. As soon as they heard it they knew and might say, "Farmer Jones is on his way into town." It was the same with horses; each one has a different step, and people came to recognize the sound of these steps like a policeman today can pick out fingerprints.

At last Tim broke down and confessed to his foul deed. No one knows to this day why he did what he did; this was never brought out at the trial. But there is no doubt that he never thought he'd get caught or found out. He thought he was perfectly safe.

So often you and I fool ourselves, or try to fool ourselves, into thinking we can get by with doing the wrong thing. For a time we may, but eventually we are found out, or our consciences give us such a bad time that we wish we were discovered.

Our wrongdoing speaks much more loudly than we realize. It shouts in a voice we may not hear. Medical doctors who have studied men very carefully have learned that many of the diseases from which we suffer are caused by fear, anxiety, and worry. These are germs of character which we can control.

THE YOKE

For centuries the yoke has been used as an aid in heavy pulling or carrying. A yoke is a frame, or a bar of wood carved to fit the shoulders either of some animal or a man. The yoke can either be single or double. The double yoke harnesses two animals together in order that their combined strength can be exerted in the drawing of a cart, a plow, or any other object.

The yoke also has been a symbol of bondage or servitude, or subjection. At one time it was held over the heads of slaves in the market to indicate their position.

But the yoke also has other symbolic values. It was and is used to describe brotherhood, showing that individuals may be bound to one another in a joint effort for good. Elton Trueblood, a professor in a midwestern college, established an organization which is called the Yokefellows. You may have seen men and women wearing the small yoke pin of membership. These people pledge themselves to give of their time, talent, and money to Christian service. They take the yoke of service gladly. To them wearing the yoke is a happy thing. They volunteer for service to others.

The yoke can indicate many things: to harness, to join, to link, to couple. It is sometimes used as a symbol of marriage. This is a yoke which people want to assume. For them, assuming this yoke is one of the aims of life. The yoke can either be a burden to carry or a joy. It depends upon the circumstances and the particular situation.

There is a very exciting story in the Old Testament about the prophet Jeremiah carrying a yoke on his shoulders through the narrow streets of Jerusalem. He did this in order to call attention to himself and the problems of his people. He was confident that these problems could only be solved by obeying the will of God, and this included taking a yoke upon themselves as a nation.

Jesus said to his followers: "Take my yoke upon you, and learn from me." This was an invitation to them to become students of his way of life. To enter into the presence of God through "the Way" he would open up to men. Accepting the yoke was a common expression in Jesus' day. It was used in reference to students who came to study under a rabbi. Therefore this meaning, when Jesus used it, was perfectly understood by those to whom he spoke.

We are invited to accept the yoke of the Master and try to live his way of life in our present-day world. This may seem difficult to some. Others may refer to it as a sort of slavery. However, there is no slavery when a person voluntarily chooses to do something.

Jesus said that his yoke was easy to bear, that it would rest lightly. Truly, that is the way it seems when one begins to realize the satisfactions of being a follower of the Way.

~~~~~~~SIR RICHARD~~~~~~~

Did you ever hear of Dick Whittington? Perhaps you have, perhaps you haven't, but surely your parents have. If you would ask them about this they might answer, "Yes, I've heard the name. I think that it comes from an old English tale." But they'd be only half right. There have been many stories about him. Dick Whittington was a real man, born about 1358, and this story of his life is true. If one day you visit London you may see a great hospital in Smithfield called St. Bartholomew's which Dick built when he became Sir Richard Whittington.

He was a very little boy when he left his home county of Lancashire to make his fortune in the great city of London. His mother and father had died, and Dick was left alone without any money, relatives, or friends. He found a poor, starving, homeless, little kitten one day, and it became his companion on the road to London.

Dick was fortunate and found a job as a scullery boy— that is, washing pots and pans in a room off the kitchen of a great house. The master of the house was a merchant with many ships going to all parts of the world. He was a kind man and often would give his servants a chance to make a little extra money by sending anything they wished on one of his ships. This would be traded if possible, and whatever profit was made came back to the servant.

Shortly after Dick came to work in the house a ship was to sail down the coast of Africa. Dick had nothing to offer; all he owned was his cat. So he gave the cat into the care of the captain. After parting with his pet everything seemed to go wrong. The cook often beat him, so he made up his mind to go back to Lancashire.

He came to the village of Holloway and was tired. He lay down at the side of the road and went to sleep, and when he awoke he heard the Bells of Bow ringing. They seemed to be saying "Turn-back-Whitt-ing-ton-thrice-Lord-Mayor-of-London." The thought seemed so funny to Dick that he began to laugh. But he got the message: when things don't go the way you want them to, or when someone doesn't like you, when things are hard, you should not crawl into a corner and cry about it, or run away, but face your problem head on.

Dick got up and started back for his master's house. When he arrived, what do you think? You're right! The ship had returned with the news that Dick's cat had been sold for a large sum of money. It seems that when the ship had put into an African port to trade, the king of that particular area had invited the captain and his officers to a meal. The place was overrun with mice. They were into everything, even running over the food. The captain sent a man to the ship to get the cat. It must have been a rare sight to see what the cat did with the mice. The king, of course, wanted the cat for his own and offered six bags filled with gold.

This gold became the foundation for a huge fortune. The

master kept the gold and reinvested some of it for his little scullery boy and showed him how to take care of it himself. Bit by bit the poor boy built himself fame and fortune. The bells were right—Dick Whittington did serve three terms as mayor of the city of London.

____BLUEBERRY HILL____

In Brookfield, New Hampshire, is a mountain known as Tibbetts Hill. From the top of it you can get a magnificent view of the White and Green Mountains. Several years ago a man began clearing the top of Tibbetts Hill, removing all the trees and brush. It was a backbreaking job, but he continued to do it, a bit more each year.

After it had been cleared, the whole area was burned over. This may sound easy, but it is not, for great care must be taken in order that the fires be kept under control at all times. It is done in the spring, before the snow melts at the edges of the clearing. Oil is sprayed over the ground and set on fire. A year later little blueberry plants begin to come up. After another year they bear fruit.

It would be so wounderful if this were all, and the farmer then simply picked the berries. But not so. There must be a constant war waged upon weeds and other berry-bearing plants. This can't be done by wholesale spraying but must be a pinpoint operation. Wholesale spraying would kill off the blueberries as well as the unwanted plants. Each year starlings flock down by the thousands. They could eat all the berries on a twenty-five acre plot in almost the time that it takes you to clap your hands. Traps must be set and baited with grain every night. Sometimes at the end of the next day, as many as two or three hundred birds will be taken from each trap.

There are also other little enemies. You've often seen an inchworm. He appears to be a nice little fellow. He hunches up his back, then stretches out his front end and moves along, not an inch but a fraction of an inch at a time. Surely, you say, he could not be a problem. He wouldn't be if he didn't like blueberries so well. He likes them perhaps even better than you do. The inchworm moves slowly, but a mass, a pack, or a horde of them, whatever they are called in a large number, can destroy a huge patch of berries in a night.

When the berries are ready for picking in August, boys from neighboring villages come to "rake" them, with scoops that look like dustpans with long fingers close together along one side. This is very hard work, and only a small area can be picked over in a day.

When the berries have been harvested, they cannot be sent directly to stores. They are trucked to Gorham, New Hampshire, where they are carefully cleaned by blowing controlled blasts of air over the berries. This moving air carries the leaves and twigs away. Then the berries must be washed. During this washing process the unripened berries are removed. The green berries float to the top.

Again the berries are loaded onto trucks for a trip to the processing plant, where they are packaged to be sold as either fresh or frozen fruit. Now they are ready for shipment to Detroit, Chicago, New York City, the West Coast, anywhere you happen to live, so that your mother may serve them to you for breakfast in bowls, or in muffins, or pancakes.

or however you like them best. You may even eat some that are dehydrated and packaged with cereal.

What a lot of work there must be in order that you may enjoy some blueberries. The word that best describes this whole process is "persistence." Nothing worthwhile is accomplished without persistence. We get an idea. It doesn't happen just because we think it, or would like it to, without persistence. It takes work and more work.

It would be easy, when the starlings and the inchworms come, to say, "Let boys and girls do without blueberries." But no, you can eat and enjoy them because some men, women, boys, and girls have been persistent.

THE NOBLE DUKE

There was once a duke who, in fun, is remembered as "the noble Duke of York" because he could never make up his mind. You have known boys and girls who could never make up their minds. One moment, "Let's play this," and five minutes later, "I don't want to play that anymore, let's play this instead." This goes on all the time. It is not that they necessarily get tired of a game quickly, but rather they don't know their own minds.

There is a song that was made up about the Duke of York which is still sung in England. It tells how the duke was in command of a thousand men. He marched them up a hill but when he got them there he didn't know what to do with them so he marched them down again. When he got to the bottom of the hill, he still didn't know what to do, so he marched them halfway up the hill again. The song says that then they were "neither up nor down."

Back in 1884 a split developed in the Republican party. There was a group who would not support James G. Blaine for the presidency. Those who remained true to the party made fun of those who had deserted and said that those who had bolted the ranks did so because they felt themselves superior. They called the deserters Mugwumps from an Indian word meaning "great men." These people didn't really feel superior, they simply didn't know their own minds. So mugwump came to mean someone who sat on a fence, with half of him on one side and half on the other. Albert J. Engle, who was a member of the House of Representatives is quoted as saying: "a mugwump has his mug on one side of the political fence and his wump on the other."

There was once a man who lived in Northampton, England, who would attend Anglican Church one Sunday and the Methodist Church the next. The people of the Anglican Church invited him to join their church, and the Methodist people invited him to become a member of theirs, but he could never make up his mind. When he died, his wife wanted his body buried in the Anglican churchyard. Church officials didn't think this was quite right. If you visit this churchyard today, you will find his body buried so that half of it is inside the fence and half outside.

There is a story about a couple who wanted to be married and went to a minister. "Wilt thou have this woman to be thy wedded wife?" said the clergyman.

"Ya, ya, I suppose so."

"You must answer, I will."

"Ya, I suppose so," the man replied.

"No," insisted the minister, "You must . . ."

"Now look here," said the bride, "you'll have him saying he won't in a moment if you keep badgering him."

Perhaps it is not easy, but it is a virtue to learn to quickly weigh a problem or a situation and then come to a definite conclusion. This type of action on the part of a person often makes the difference between success and failure. Sometimes our decisions may not be right, but people will know that we can be depended upon and they will trust us.

WE WOULD BE
BUILDING

Have you ever played in the sand building castles? With a little care it is possible to mold a little sand into many shapes. Some people are even called sand sculptors. The sand of the lakeshore can be fun, but the sand of the seashore can be even more so, it seems.

You may remember that when you were a tiny child, you built things from blocks in the nursery. At first you were not very good and found it most difficult to get the blocks in right balance so they could be piled up in the way you wanted to place them. When they came tumbling down at times you would be so frustrated that you simply couldn't help but cry. But you would try again and again, and at last you would achieve success. Uncomfortable as these experiences were, they all added to your growth. You learned that with real effort you could accomplish what you wanted to do.

Grown people often speak of "dream castles." By this they mean that in quiet moments they think of those things they would like to do and in their mind's eye see their desires become a reality. Perhaps even the whole process of thinking might be conceived as building dream castles.

Purd Eugene Dietz wrote a wonderful hymn: "We Would Be Building." Dr. Dietz is a well-known clergyman of the United Church of Christ. At the time he wrote this hymn he was minister of the Trinity Evangelical and Reformed Church in Philadelphia. This hymn was included in a program of the Christian Youth Council at Lakeside, Ohio, and in 1936 printed in a book of devotions called **Follow Me.** Almost overnight it became one of the best-known hymns in America.

Dr. Dietz tells us he was doing graduate work in Edinburgh during the winter 1931–32 and there, for the first time, heard Sibelius' great melody from "Finlandia" used as a hymn tune. He bought a copy of the Scottish Hymnary in order to have the arrangement. In 1934-35 there were a series of conferences held in the United States on the general theme "Christian Youth Building a New World." One night he composed words which developed the theme of these conferences to be sung to the tune "Finlandia." The hymn suggests the need for building and repair in the Christian church, if it is to take its proper place in the new world. We must have visions, dreams of what a new world under Christ can be, then work to make those dreams a reality.

The Master told of two men, one who built his house on the sand and another who built his house on a rock. The winds and the rains lashed at the house that was built upon the sand; the foundations were washed away and the house collapsed. The house built upon the stone withstood the onslaughts of the elements and remained. The suggestion was of course, that we need to build our spiritual houses upon strong rocks of faith.

~~~~PASSACONAWAY~~~~

Passaconaway was a Penacook Indian who lived at the time the English were pushing their way out from Boston and Salem and settling villages and towns. He was a very wise man and lived to a ripe old age. Some historians think he lived to be at least one hundred years old. He was a medicine man and a warrior of great strength. No man of the tribe could use as heavy a bow as Passaconaway. An early story tells us that this wonderful man had powers so strong that he could make water burn, rocks move on the hillsides without touching them, trees dance, and could actually turn himself into a flaming tree. This same story relates that his greatest feat was to take dried leaves in the winter time, burn them to ash, and cast them upon water, where they would become leaves again.

Perhaps the greatest contribution that Passaconaway made was his last speech to his people. There have been many famous speeches for which men will ever be remembered. Lincoln's Gettysburg Address is one we are taught in school and often required to memorize. The apostle Paul gave a memorable address to the people in Athens. Peter's speech on the day of Pentecost is also one that is worth knowing by heart.

Passaconaway learned many lessons from life, but one lesson was most important of all. His speech is one which might well be listened to again and again by our modern world. Said the medicine man: "I am a great oak that has withstood the storms of more than a hundred winters. My eyes are dim—my limbs totter—I soon must fall. But when I was young and sturdy no man could bend my bow. When my arrows could pierce a deer at a hundred yards, when I could bury my hatchet in a sapling no larger than a lodge pole, then I delighted in war. The English came and took our lands. I made war against them—I tried witchcraft—I talked with the Great Spirit. The Great Spirit has said to me: 'Tell your people, peace, peace is the only hope of your race.' "

Mankind has forever glorified warfare, and yet warfare has never settled anything. Each generation has had its wars, and all they have done is create distrust and hatred.

Passaconaway simply restated the words of Jesus when he said: "My peace I leave with you!" "Peace, peace with all men is the command of the Great Spirit," said he, "and peace is the last wish of Passaconaway."

CONSCIENCE

There is in each one of us something that we call our conscience. This something bothers us when we do what we know we should not have done, or when we fail to do that which we should do. Sometimes our conscience just pricks and bothers us, while at other times it can do fearsome things with us. It can fill us with fear. It can arouse great feelings of guilt.

In the White Mountains of New Hampshire you may someday see a little stream which is named "Nancy's Brook." Who was Nancy? She was a servant girl who worked for a man named Captain Harrison of Riverton, New Hampshire. Nancy fell in love with a boy named Jim Swindell, who also worked for this captain. They became engaged. When they made plans to go to Portsmouth to be married, Nancy entrusted all her savings to Jim. While Nancy and Mrs. Harrison were on a shopping trip to Lancaster, Jim left the farm and started for Portsmouth alone, of course taking all Nancy's life savings with him.

On returning to the farm, Nancy heard of his desertion. She

told her master and mistress that she was going to follow the boy and try to catch up with him before he got to Portsmouth. It was December, and the ground was covered with snow. The Harrisons tried desperately to persuade her to change her mind, but she was determined to go.

The closest settlement was many miles away. The wind was blowing from the northwest and the air filled with snow. She tied her few belongings into a small bundle and set out to try to overtake her faithless lover. There was no road, only a blazed trail through the mountains. She thought that by walking very fast she would find him camping in Crawford Notch, so she pushed on through the night. Finally she came to the spot where Jim Swindell had camped and found the ashes of his night's fire beginning to cool. Desperately she tried to fan the embers into flame, but was unable. On she went, cold and hungry. She climbed the wild pass and started to follow the river down toward Conway.

After hours of desperate effort Nancy gave up. A searching party sent out by the Harrisons found her body on the bank of a little stream, frozen stiff in the snow. Ever since that stream has carried her name.

But that is not the end of the story. We started thinking about this thing called conscience. When Jim Swindell learned of what had happened to his former sweetheart, he laughed as if it were a big joke that a girl could be so foolish. But he had not counted upon his conscience. It began to bother him. What he had done worked on his mind so much that finally he went completely insane and ran off into the mountains and was never heard from again. For years, even today, some people will tell you that on cold, still winter nights the mountain walls above Nancy's Brook will echo the groans of the ghost of this faithless lover as he cries in anguish for his deeds.

DO UNTO OTHERS

Jesus once said to his disciples: "Whatever you wish that men would do to you, do so to them." To many people these are nice words to repeat, but they don't pay too much attention to the meaning and act as if this simply were not true. People are selfish, mean, unkind, and then wonder why others are selfish, mean and unkind toward them.

In the White Mountains, in the time of the Revolution, there was a man who was one of the largest landowners in the area at that time. He was one of the first real estate promoters. His only interest was making money, and he didn't care how he did it. At one time he owned the entire Jefferson township. This land he sold off through the use of one promotional scheme after another.

One year there was great scarcity of crops in the mountains and the settlers faced a hard winter. However, Colonel Whipple had suffcient land so that even though the crops were sparse, he was able to harvest enough grain for himself and some which he could have easily shared with his neighbors. This he refused to do. His attitude was that if folks were starving, it was not a responsibility of his, and for all he cared they could be hungry.

A group of people from Bartlett, knowing that the colonel had food stored, trudged through the pass in the mountains to beg him to sell them a small amount of grain in order that their children might live. They had dragged small sleds behind them on which they had hoped to be able to haul some food back to their settlement.

Beg as they might, he would not hear their requests. The children could eat their shoes if they were hungry was his attitude. Finally, after long pleading, the settlers appeared to be defeated. They started away as if to go again to their homes. However, they did not go far from the colonel's farm and hid out for the rest of the day. Night came, but they did not move from their place of hiding until they felt sure that the Whipple household was all fast asleep. Cautiously they made their way back to the farmstead, careful not to break so much as a twig or let the snow crunch under their feet.

One by one they crawled underneath the granary. With a sharp knife one of the party cut a hole through the floor, and the grain began to run out. How many sacks of grain they took no one knows, but it was sufficient to keep the little group from Bartlett alive until springtime.

It wasn't until some days later that the colonel became aware that his supply of grain had become very much depleted. At first he couldn't understand what had happened, but then after careful examination he found the hole in the floor which had been plugged with a piece of wood. Of course he was very angry, but this did him no good. What had happened was his own fault. He had no one else to blame. Had he only thought in terms of doing to others as he wanted them to do to him, he would have been paid for his grain and gained the everlasting love and appreciation of the people. Instead, even today his name is loathed.

——SERMONS IN STONE——

At Stone Mountain in Georgia and in the heart of the Black Hills of South Dakota, men have carved giant statues on the face of mountains. These magnificent sculptures depict famous characters in the history of the United States. They are inspirations to all who see them. We marvel at the ingenuity and skill of men which permit them to shape the rock. We are excited by the thoughts of the men who are pictured here who have inspired their fellow men to do great things.

However, long before men conceived the idea of cutting and shaping stone, God had been carving sermons in stone. The story of the earth is to be read in his handiwork. Geologists can tell us the condition and shape of the world hundreds and thousands of years ago simply by looking at the rocks which the master hand has moved and marked.

We are told in the Old Testament that God created man out of the dust of the earth. God also memorialized his creation by carving his features in the stones. Nathaniel Hawthorne was inspired by the "Old Man of the Mountain," a wonderful portrait of a man's face which God carved on the side of Cannon Mountain. We believe that the first white man to see this face was Nathaniel Hall, who with others was working on the building of a road through the wilderness. There are at least two stories of his discovery; either one of them might be correct. One of these stories tells us that he had gone to get a drink of water from the pond at the foot of the mountain. He happened to look up and called to his fellow workers that he had seen the face of God. Another story states that two workmen were washing in the lake and seeing the "Old Man," thought someone had been there before them and carved the rock. They were right and wrong. It was carved, but not by a human.

The Indians had long held this face in awe, and legend says that only chiefs of the tribe were permitted to look at it, and then only in time of great peril to the tribe.

Another marvelous story about this natural rock carving known as the Great Stone Face is a beautiful one woven about an Italian painter who wanted to paint a picture of the Christ sitting in judgment, but could find no subject to sit as a model. A dying priest who knew of his search left word that in the wilderness of the White Mountains he would find an inspiration. He journeyed to America and in Quebec secured an Indian guide and woodsman to lead him. At last, after long, hard travel, he came to a beautiful valley and the shores of a lovely little lake. The Indian pointed upward, and there the painter beheld the face for which he had long sought. He at once set up camp and sketched and painted until he finally produced his greatest work, "The Judging Christ."

People look at you, expecting to read something in your face; will what they read be good and inspiring, or will they find gloom and discomfort? It is entirely up to you.

111

⁓WANTING SOMETHING⁓

There is a lovely story that comes down in the traditions of the Penacook Indians. A young man fell in love with a beautiful young woman, as young men often do. She accepted his hand when he proposed marriage. The day was set, but it turned into a day of sadness rather than a day of joy, for the young woman became ill and died. The Indian boy was heartsick. Someone had told him a story of the "Island of Souls" and that if he sought for it, he could find a pathway which would lead him there where he would find his lost love.

Being a brave young man and very much in love, he set out to find this wonderful, mysterious island. For days he traveled through the deep snow, until finally he found himself descending from the mountains to a flat land. Weeks and months later, in a strange land he came to the lodge of a very old man. This old man had long white hair and his eyes blazed.

"Yes," he told the young brave, "there is an Island of Souls and you are going in the right direction. Farther on to

112

the south, you will find a land of scrub pine and sand. It is a harsh land, and the heat of the sun will burn your flesh. But if you keep going you will find the Island of Souls."

The young man toiled on even though his feet were bleeding and torn. At last he came to a great gulf. The water was heavenly blue and seemed to be filled with all kinds of wondrous fish. On the shore he saw a lovely canoe. It looked strong and light. The young man didn't remember ever having seen such a wonderful example of workmanship. Truly it could have been made only by the Great Spirit. He knew he was on the right path because the old man had told him he would find it.

Paddling out into the gulf was a new experience. He tasted the water and found it very salty. Suddenly he became aware of another canoe alongside. In it was the girl whom he sought. They were going on together to the Island of Souls. Very suddenly a storm arose. It was difficult to keep their crafts afloat. They looked down through the clear water, and below them saw the bodies of others who had not been able to pass through the waves. But the Great Spirit, who had been watching their progress, knew they had pure souls and were good and so protected them, and they continued their journey until they at last reached the Island of Souls.

Never had they seen anything like it. Long, white sand beaches, trees with strange feathery leaves, lovely flowers in profusion—so different from the land of snows. The two lovers were about to step ashore when the Great Spirit approached them and told the young man he could not stay, that his task in the land of snows had not been finished; therefore, he had to return and stay until he had done the work which the Great Spirit wanted him to do. But the Great Spirit told him that, in time, if he lived as a strong, good man, he might come back and be at home on the Island of Souls.

Sadly the brave turned back and journeyed to the land of

ice and snow, knowing that in the eyes of the Great Spirit he was not ready for the Island of Souls. He lived as strong and good men should and became a chief, loved by his people.

So often we want something that we've not earned. We want something before we are ready, prepared to receive. We too must spend our time in the land of ice and snow, until that day when we can live on the Island of Souls.

HOPE

You and I have a lot to eat. We have warm homes and we are comfortable.

It is hard for us to understand how difficult and uncomfortable things were for the people who settled our country. It makes no difference what part of this country you think about; east, west, north, or south, the folks who settled it suffered.

The settlers of the Dakota prairies had such hardships that we are apt to shudder with fear when we read or hear about them. A family named Wilson lived near the town of Redfield, South Dakota. All summer the Wilsons had worked hard to store up enough food to last through the winter. Then fire destroyed their little shack and all the food they had so carefully gathered. It began to snow and didn't stop until the great plains had been blanketed with several feet of the fleecy crystals. The Wilsons crawled into a hole which they had dug for a garbage pit, and there they lived through the winter months with hardly anything to eat but dried peas.

Near the little town of Princeton, Minnesota, lived a family named Flemming. In the fall a bear ate up or destroyed all the food they had stored for the winter. Occasionally Mr. Flemming was able to catch a rabbit, and each day he struggled to dig up cattails from the frozen earth so his family would survive.

In New England the winter of 1777 was very harsh. People lost their horses as they tried to find their way into settlements. A strange story comes to us about a horse near Bartlett. The snow was so heavy it bent the trees over, forming snow caves. There is nothing unusual about these formations, but this horse trapped in one of these snow caves managed to find enough to graze on, so that he lived through the winter.

In 1790, when Joseph Hinkham moved into the area of Jackson, New Hampshire, the snow was already many feet deep. The nearest grist mill was ten miles away, and Mr. Hinkham and the other pioneers had to trudge all this distance carrying bushels of corn on their shoulders if they wanted it ground into meal.

It is recorded that at the time when people were trying to settle the area which is now Bethlehem, New Hampshire, their food ran short. When famine threatened a community such as this, it was often necessary for folks to walk fifty or sixty miles to get supplies. Some of the men from Bethlehem walked a total of 377 miles, all the way to Concord, Massachusetts, and back dragging sleds behind them. It took them four full weeks. When they returned they found some of the hardy folks were still alive. They had eaten tree roots, some of which they had boiled with a moccasin, others with powder horns to give a little flavor to the broth.

Many people in those days wore heavy belts made from animal skins. As they became thinner and more and more emaciated, they would draw their belts a little tighter thinking this helped them feel the hunger a little less.

Why did people do all these things? Why did they leave England to settle our eastern coast? Why did they leave settled Massachusetts for the wilderness? They were all seeking something, seeking freedom, a chance to have their own land. They were ever seeking something better than what they had.

We all know the saying, "At the end of the rainbow is a pot of gold." Men are always sure that somehow they will find the kingdom of God on earth. They used to believe it was like that pot of gold, ready to be picked off the end of the rainbow, but now they realize it is going to take a long time and a lot of work. People filled with hope are anxious to keep on searching. As long as there is hope, there is a future for our human race.

___THE BLACK DRAGON___

Far back in the mountains of Transylvania lies a beautiful medieval village surrounded by a massive wall which, in some places, is twenty feet thick. In the heart of the town a solid stone tower stands like a gigantic finger pointing upward.

Near the center of the village there is a lovely inn built hundreds of years ago, but still in excellent condition. Before the Second World War very few people from the outside had ever visited this place, not because it was difficult to find but because folks just hadn't wanted to go there.

It had been thought that this village might become a fine summer resort, but the idea failed. People heard strange stories: that the mountains were too rugged to climb, that some people had never returned. However, what did the most damage to the reputation of the village were stories of the black dragon. It was said this dragon was responsible for the disappearance of many people.

The story of the discovery of this black dragon is thrilling. Through a strange chain of circumstances, an adventurous young man and young woman both happened to be staying at the village inn at the same time. Naturally they heard the dragon stories. With the rashness of youth they set forth, like St. George of old, to find and, if possible, to kill this dangerous black dragon.

Day after day they toured and explored. They discovered the mountains were honeycombed with caves. They questioned the villagers over and over again and finally learned the black dragon made his home in one of these caves. When they eventually found the correct cave, they courageously entered and were shocked to find all over the floor of the cave gruesome relics, bones of people who had previously investigated the dragon's home.

Tradition said that the dragon lived far back in the cave and the only way to arouse him was to throw rocks into a deep hole that was there. Although they were afraid, these young people were brave and continued to visit the cave daily; but they heard nothing and saw nothing. The only thing of which they were aware was the heat and the dampness. Finally one day they decided to throw rocks into the hole to see if they could arouse the fearsome animal. They dropped a rock and waited and listened. For quite a time nothing happened. Then they cast in a larger rock, and in just a few seconds there was a soft hissing sound. Not waiting to see what was coming, they ran for the entrance. In a moment the hissing turned into a roar like that of a thousand lions. They had hardly reached the mouth of the cave when great clouds of steam billowed out. Then tons of hot water gushed forth. The black dragon had been found and killed.

A subterranean stream of boiling water flowed at the bottom of the well within the cave. When people threw in stones they plugged up the natural outlet and the water, having no other place to go, gushed upward. Many had been killed because they hadn't run fast enough to escape the steam.

The black dragon was not the cloud of steam. The black dragon was not the hot water. The black dragon was fear of the unknown. Fear is probably the worst enemy a human being has to fight. Fear causes us to do things we should not do. Fear keeps us from doing those things we should do. Fear can even make us ill. It is easy for folks to tell us not to be afraid, but it isn't easy for us to take their advice. We must always try to learn what is making us afraid—who or what the black dragon really is, so we may find and destroy it.

NUTS

When I was a little boy my mother would often say to me; "A stitch in time saves nine!" I don't think I really knew what it meant, but as I grew older I gradually began to understand.

Recently I went out into our back yard. There, sitting on the fence, was a squirrel, a pretty squirrel with a long, bushy tail which he held gracefully. I said; "Why hello, Mr. Squirrel, what are you up to?"

He looked at me rather disdainfully and replied, "Nuts!"

"Why Mr. Squirrel," I said, "that's not very gentlemanly of you to speak in that way."

"Why not?" he asked. "You asked what I was doing and I told you, nuts. I'm gathering nuts as you can easily see if you'll take the trouble to look." With this, the saucy little squirrel ran along the fence and with a mighty jump landed on the ground several feet away, where there were a large number of acorns. He picked up several of them, making his little cheeks bulge, and then went off to his home.

Do you save anything? I expect that some of you when

you were born had grandparents who started a savings account for you in a nearby bank. But do you keep putting pennies, dimes, or quarters in it, or do you spend all of your coins for bubble gum or comic books? Saving is a habit that is very good, but many people today have forgotten this and spend everything they earn, feeling that if they get in need someone will take care of them.

The little squirrel returned shortly and sat looking at me for a moment. Then he laughed. "Don't you save?" he asked. "Or are you like many of your kind, just a sponger?"

"Certainly I try to save," I replied.

"Well, you don't seem to be working very hard!" said he, and dashed away with some more acorns. I feel pretty certain that this little friend of mine will not go hungry during the winter months; he has taken care to see that he will have an abundance of food.

Jesus said, "Do not lay up for yourselves treasures on earth." But by that he didn't mean that we should not be prudent. Some people give their whole energy simply to collecting, with no thought of doing good or helping others. These people wouldn't like to be called misers, but that's what they really are. It is these of whom Jesus was speaking. All through the Gospels the Master recommended generosity and giving. You cannot give unless you have a store out of which to give. We are told in the New Testament that we should lay up treasures in heaven. This is done by doing kind things and giving love, and by caring for those who honestly are unable to care for themselves—little children and older people who simply no longer have the physical strength. Save in the bank for a time of need; save in God's storehouse too.

POISON IVY

"Rhus toxicodendron" is the name of a very lovely plant which has three leaves in a cluster. Sometimes it grows along the ground. At other times it climbs over stone walls or up fences. In the spring and during the summer the leaves are a beautiful green, and in the fall these leaves may turn a wonderful red. In the southern states it may grow as an upright shrub, or twine around trunks of trees. On Appledore Island off Portsmouth, New Hampshire, and certain parts of California, it sometimes grows eight or ten feet tall. It has whitish, berrylike fruit. It is a most attractive plant. Often this plant is confused with the Virginia creeper, which has larger leaves and five of them rather than three in the cluster.

This lovely plant has names other than "Rhus toxicodendron." It is called poison ivy or poison oak. Many people who come in contact with it have some very painful results. The skin becomes inflamed, and little blisters appear which itch frightfully. If you scratch, the blisters break and the watery substance from the blisters makes your arms or legs wet—you look awful and you are miserable.

123

Dandelions are very pretty. The flowers are yellow and bright. Their leaves are notched and vivid green. The leaves are good to eat in the springtime, and many people pick them. When the dandelion goes to seed, it is also beautiful as the yellow flower changes into a crown of white. But, if permitted, dandelions will take over a lawn, killing the grass. It becomes a great nuisance for your father.

Many things in life are not good for us or are harmful to others, and yet seem to be so very attractive and lovely. Sin is doing those things that we should not do or not doing the things we should do. Often sin appears attractive. Many times it is much more fun doing those things we should not do, and so we do them without thinking of the results for ourselves and for others, and often we do not care. It is much easier to leave undone those things that we should do.

Poison ivy, like sin, is unpredictable. There are times when it appears to do no harm at all. People will often say, "I'm immune to it." This is a way of saying that they appear to receive no harmful effects from being near or coming into contact with it. Then all of a sudden, without warning, their skin becomes red and itchy. They no longer are immune. Often it seems that we can do things we know we should not do and get by with it. Many times we do not do the things we should, and there appear to be no harmful results. But, as with poison ivy, there may come a time when the wrong we do, or the things we should do and leave undone, result in great unhappiness or endanger ourselves or others.

It is best to learn to recognize poison ivy, then keep away from it. It doesn't pay to take chances. It is the same with sin.

WHAT ARE YOU TALKING ABOUT?

A teacher in church school one Sunday said to the children, "Please stop talking!" At once the room became quiet, so quiet, in fact, you could have heard a pin drop. If you had walked in, you would have said that everyone had stopped talking. Did they?

For many years in Danvers, Massachusetts, there has been a home for people who are blind, deaf, and dumb. One day a mother and father took their little boy with them when they went to visit in this home. One old lady, who had lost her sight and hearing and was unable to talk, placed her hand on the little boy's head, held up four fingers, then put her hand in the hand of another guest at the home, and began to move her fingers rapidly. Her friend, who couldn't see but could hear, speak, and feel, immediately began to translate the movement of the hand into spoken words that the mother and father could understand. This wonderful old woman then told the age of the boy, his height, and many other things that she had learned through touching the child.

Do you think that the boys and girls in the class had stopped talking? Of course they hadn't. You may have heard that actions speak louder than words. They were not moving their lips, but they were moving their eyes, their hands, and their feet. All these movements were telling many things.

We say that a book speaks. It has no voice, but it tells many things. We say that God speaks; he does, but perhaps not in spoken words such as you and I use. A look says many things. Did you ever say, "I know he doesn't like me, I can tell by the way he looks." Did you ever see a boy with dirty fingernails, or a girl who looks as if she never washes her face? Surely you have. These things tell you much more than words spoken with the voice could do.

As you ride along the road with your parents, you see signboards on which pictures or words are printed. These signboards speak. Do you keep your bedroom clean and straight? Anyone looking at the room can tell much about you, because the room speaks very loud and clear.

The books and the magazines that a person has lying around his home talk, talk about the kind of person who lives there. The things you read, the radio and TV programs you watch, tell much more about you than you'd be apt to admit.

Your actions tell a lot about you, too; they speak loud. If you smile, you speak, and people will answer you with a smile. If you walk around with a long face, or your face all screwed up as if you had been drinking vinegar, you can expect a sour answer to your unspoken words.

What are you saying?

~~A GREAT CHRISTIAN~~

If you visit St. Patrick's Cathedral in Dublin, Ireland, you will find that it is a Roman Catholic church; but if you go to St. Patrick's Cathedral in Belfast, you will learn that it is a Protestant church. Patrick was neither Roman Catholic nor Protestant. Everyone thinks of him as an Irishman. Perhaps he was by adoption, but not by birth. St. Patrick's Day on the seventeenth of March is not a celebration of this great man's birth but his death. No one knows the exact date of his birth, nor the place. Yet there is much we do know about him, the most important being that he was a good Christian.

He was born in the fourth century, perhaps in the south-western part of England. It is known that he was the son of a practicing Christian, a leader among a group of Christians, probably what we today would call an evangelical church.

When Patrick was about sixteen years old he was captured by Irish pirates who carried him off as a slave. He was taken to a place which is now known as Connacht. Here he was forced to care for pigs, and continued this for six long years. It was during this time he began to feel great faith in the power of God and day after day prayed for deliverance. At last, we don't know exactly how, he was able to escape. He found a ship ready to sail and after considerable coaxing secured a berth aboard. He was confident that all this came as the result of prayer.

Aboard the ship were a number of Irish hounds. These animals were very fierce and unmanageable, but Patrick seemed to have a way with them, and they responded to him much as we are told the birds and animals did to St. Francis of Assisi.

After several days' voyage, the ship put into port on the French coast. Patrick could have continued to sail with this ship because of his way with the dogs, but he wanted no more of his companions and so left the ship. After a time he found a home on a quiet little island in the Mediterranean, and it was many years until he at last returned to England. It was after his return to his homeland that he had a vision, like Paul of old when he saw a man from Macedonia who said to him, "Come over and help us." Patrick's call seemed to summon him to Ireland, back to where he had been a slave. Before going, however, he went to France to study and prepare to serve as a Christian missionary.

For twenty-nine years, until his death, March 17, 461, Patrick worked in Ireland. He did many things, but most of his time was given to preaching the way to God. He never wavered from his complete faith and his belief that God had chosen him for the particular purpose of preaching his love.

There are many stories told about Patrick. Perhaps some of them are not true, but they serve to indicate how highly he became respected and loved by the people whom he served. He was dauntless, and nothing could turn him away from the Christ whom he loved and whose lessons he tried to teach.